With Great Respect and Love

Yoga Sutras
of Patanjali

interpreted by
Mukunda Stiles

WEISER BOOKS
Boston, MA/York Beach, ME

First published in 2002 by
Red Wheel/Weiser, LLC
368 Congress Street
Boston, MA 02210

Library of Congress Cataloging-in-Publication Data
Patañjali.
    [Yogasutra. English]
    Yoga sutras of patanjali /Mukunda Stiles.
    p. cm.
    Includes bibliographical references.
    ISBN 1-57863-201-3 (pbk. : alk. paper)
    I. Yoga—Early works to 1800. I. Title.
B132.Y6 P263 2002
181'.452—dc21

2001026516

Typeset in 11.5 Centaur
Illustration of Patanjali provided courtesy of B. K. S. Iyengar.

PRINTED IN CANADA

TCP

08 07 06 05 04 03 02 01
8 7 6 5 4 3 2 1

Contents

Sanskrit Text with Word-by-Word Translation

Sources

Invocation to the Lord of Yoga*

ॐ

My own True Self you are!
  My intellect is Your consort.
The life force of my *pranas* are Your attendants.
  My body is my Lord's sacred temple.
All my senses worship You in all forms.
  My sleep is but absorption into Your Spirit.
Wherever I go, I am immersed in Your form
  All my words are hymns in which I sing Your praises.
Any action that I do is an act of devotion to You.

Though I may have caused pain
  With the actions of my limbs; and
Though I may have brought about suffering
  With my mind or senses;
Though I may have acted in ignorance against Your Truth,
  For all these mistakes, please forgive me.
You who are the ocean of mercy.

  Sadgurunath Maharaj ki Jay —
    Victory to the True Self
  Jagadambe Mata ki Jay —
    Salutations to the Divine Mother

---

*Sutras 4 & 5 of *Shiva Manasa Puja*, paraphrased by Mukunda Stiles.

Preface

‑‑‑‑

Another *Yoga Sutra* book? Yes, there is growing interest in other perspectives on this remarkable treatise that seeks to aid in our self-knowledge and help us understand the cycle of how we swing between comfort and suffering. This book offers an interpretation especially written for students of yoga, for those who seek to transform themselves using yoga as an evolutionary path. It is written for serious thinkers who want to understand what it means to love yoga and who want to discover where they can go through dedicated regular practice.

The interpretation I give here is based on personal yoga experience gained from over thirty years of spiritual practice (*sadhana*) rather than merely philosophical understanding. My intention is to make this text easily accessible to readers without the need for an advanced course in Indian philosophy or Sanskrit. It is delivered in poetic phrasing so that it can be received more readily by the right side of the brain, unlike prose, which tends to go to the left side. To facilitate understanding, I have chosen to use common English phrasing and remove philosophical and technical Sanskrit terms. I present a version free of the normal commentary to allow readers to explore their own ideas and actively engage their inner selves in contemplative dialog. I highly recommend regular reading of this text as a way of comprehending the deeper meanings that reflection and internal dialog can bring. This is in line with the perspective on *samyama*—the continuum of contemplation (*dharana*), meditation (*dhyana*), and spiritual absorption (*samadhi*)—described by Patanjali in chapter 3.

While not a formal Sanskrit scholar, I have been a persistent practitioner of yoga and a student of the *Yoga Sutras* for over thirty years. My principal studies in the *Sutras* have been both academic (writing an undergraduate thesis on Patanjali) and spiritual (studying with my mentors Swami Shyam of Kulu, Swami Muktananda of Ganeshpuri, and Swami Prakashananda of Suptashring Devi). My interpretations of the original Sanskrit are drawn principally from available word-by-word translations of the original text. I encourage you to consult the literal translations of Sanskrit phrases in order to appreciate the task of understanding this terse Sanskrit method of presentation. My sources are cited in the last section of the book. My intention throughout the book is to convey the essence of the *Yoga Sutras* as they apply to students of yogameditation as a spiritual practice (*sadhana*), so that through them you may know yourself more fully and become of greater service to others.

Introduction

⌐

The *Yoga Sutras*, written by Maharishi Patanjali, is the original textbook of Classical Yoga. It presents the earliest complete experiential Indian philosophy for self-transformation. To speak of Yoga as merely a philosophy, however, is to trivialize its depth and scope. The *Sutras* give a detailed description of the subjective experiences associated with each stage of mindfulness, ranging from the preliminary requirements for successful practice to the most advanced intricate aspects of communion with your True Self.

CONTENT AND CONTEXT

An understanding of Patanjali's name can help you understand his unique perspective and Indian tradition. According to Vedic scholar David Frawley, Patanjali is a *bhakti*—a lover of God. As such, the Sanskrit he uses is devotional in style. I find this insight significant, and because of it, I have chosen to render my interpretation, not in prose, but in poetic phrasing. This poetic rendering, I feel, is more likely to be received in a devotional attitude (*bhava*), as I believe it was originally intended.

Patanjali's name also reveals this devotional aspect of his work. *Pata* means "falling leaves" and *anjali* refers to the "palms joined cupped in prayer." *Anjali mudra* is the name applied to the palm salutation at the heart—a common posture in depictions of Indian spiritual beings, sages, and deities. *Patanjali* thus signifies the palms harmoniously curved, cupped in a loving embrace of the fallen leaves of the *sutra* text, received from the "teacher of the most ancient teachers" and offered to the heart.

One mythological interpretation of his name is derived from another meaning of *pata*—"serpent." In this form, Patanjali is depicted as half-man, half-serpent, as shown on the cover of this book. In this guise, the lower half of Patanjali's body, rather than having legs, appears as a tail coiled three and a half times as a symbol of the latent spiritual force called *kundalini* ("coiled serpent"). The seven (or up to a thousand) heads of the serpent are arched in a posture of protection, bestowing blessings over a human torso and head. This serpent is known as *Ananta* and is the *asana* bed of Vishnu on the primordial waters. This quality of *yogasana* is referred to in sutra II, 47.

The cover image, given to me by Yogacharya B. K. S Iyengar, shows Patanjali with four arms. The front pair are in *anjali mudra*, the rear right hand holding a *chakra* (wheel) and the rear left hand holding a conch. The spirals of the conch signify infinite space out of which arises the primordial sound, *Aum*, as the origin of creation. The chakra denotes the power of the evolved mind. These are symbols traditionally associated with Vishnu, the nurturing aspect of the Lord of All. Some interpret this image of Patanjali as his transformation into a supernatural being manifesting the Lord's qualities. Thus Patanjali, as subject, has become the object of his devotional meditation. It is said that that on which we fervently meditate is what we become.

It is impossible to fix the dates of Patanjali's writing, but there are two points of view among scholars who attempt to estimate them. According to some scholars of Sanskrit treatises, the text dates from the second or third century A. D. They arrive at this conclusion by comparing the text with other philosophical works, including the *Bhagavad Gita*. Others, representing the traditional perspective, date it from the second century B. C. They base their argument on the idea that the same author also wrote an important Sanskrit grammar text, the *Mahabhashya*, which has been dated to this earlier period. Before this period, yoga ideas were found only in piecemeal manner in the writings of the *Vedas* and the *Upanishads*. References to yoga practices are found in the *Katha, Svetasvatara, Taittiriya,* and *Maitrayani Upanishads*. The *Bhagavad Gita* also describes the process of yogasana and the practice of meditation in its sixth chapter.

The *Yoga Sutras* are considered a *darshan*, literally a unique "worldview," one of six classical Indian philosophical systems. Unlike the other systems, however, Patanjali's describes not only a philosophical worldview, but also a method of awakening to and directly experiencing that worldview through self-realization. This perfected Self is, in fact, the source of this worldview. Thus, the *Sutras* present not merely a philosophy, but also a set of landmarks that chart the experiences that lead to the fullest expansion of awareness into its original nature. Darshan is also often interpreted as a mirror and it is from this perspective that Patanjali has written his aphorisms—as instruction on how to lift the veils from perception so that it may reflect the True Self.

The experiences that Patanjali describes are as valid today as they were 2000 years ago. The human mind has not changed. Thus the spiritual practice (*sadhana*) of the yogi can still help us comprehend the teachings and realize how practice unveils Spirit. Comprehension alone, however, is just another name for philosophy, something in which the mind can engage. Yoga, on the other hand, reveals yet another experience that precedes thoughts. Patanjali's Yoga aims at uncovering the source of the mind by humbly seeking what it is and inquiring, Who am I? It is the process of making your mind and your Self the object of contemplation. To put these insights into practice is to elevate yourself into a spiritual perspective, one in which thoughts and actions reflect an understanding that all of life is worthy of great love and respect. From this place, yogis begin to live a lifestyle that elevates the lives of all with whom they come into contact.

Like the Buddha three centuries before him, Patanjali sought to end suffering. Indeed, Patanjali is to Yoga what Buddha is to Buddhism. Both drew from earlier teachings to gain insight and spiritual realizations that became the hallmark of their spiritual practices. There are some overlapping points of view, and yet Patanjali's system is unique. Both Buddha and Patanjali saw the common human experience of suffering (*duhkha*) and pain, and sought to end it, first within themselves. From the insights gained in self-study, perceiving how they created or contributed to pain and suffering (both their own and others), they began to see that there are actions that must be stopped. The principal difficulty in arriving at the truth lies in removing what both called ignorance of the truth, *avidya*. In Patanjali's teachings, the practical first step of the eightfold path is to stop causing pain—to know that you not only experience pain and suffering, but also contribute to it. The second step is to desire freedom from pain, as well as from the necessity of contributing to it.

I was first introduced to the *Yoga Sutras* in the course of my studies at the University of California in 1974, at a time when my personal life was unfulfilling. I was directly experiencing the suffering that Buddha and Patanjali described. I was a motivated student in search of a release from pain. The *Sutras* caught and held my attention. They captivated my spirit and challenged my intellect. They contained many secrets that helped me to uncover and express my own hidden Self and its beauty.

The *Sutras* contain many such secrets. Students of them soon learn the variety of insights available from even a cursory reading of the many translations. Indeed, the most common formal way to study the *Sutras* is to have several translations handy in order to expose the nuances of the Sanskrit language and to appreciate the variety of views that different teachers have brought to the understanding of the text. There are translations by Indian and Sanskrit scholars like James Houghton Woods, Georg Feuerstein, and Barbara Stoler Miller; translations by hatha yogis like B. K. S. Iyengar and T. K. V. Desikachar; translations by monks like Swami Hariharananda Aranya and Swami Satchidananda; others by Vedantins like Swami Prabhavananda and his protégé Christopher Isherwood; even translations by Western psychologists like Geraldine Coster. A thorough survey of these writings reveals a wide range of perspectives and understandings. The challenge for you as a yoga student is to uncover a view that reveals personal insights that enable your *sadhana* to enrich your own life.

The sutra form of writing is aphoristic, terse, intended to convey the essence of philosophical or experiential thought in the most concise manner. The word *sutra* derives from its two component parts. *Su* means, literally, "thread or string," implying the weaving together of various views from a fundamental thought. *Tra* means "to transcend." *Sutra* thus implies the weaving of thoughts into a sequence that produces transcendental insights in your personal practice. A sustained reading of the *Sutras,* integrated with the practices described in the text, can thus yield a roadmap to your Self. This form of writing is designed to convey a wealth of inspiration that allows you to fulfill and then transcend material desires, to know, by direct experience, your spiritual nature, to expand in awareness from a limited sense of Self to a sense of the eternal True Self. Patanjali wrote the *Sutras* in the most direct manner to convey his experience of the mind. His mind was so expanded that its precise expression in the *Yoga Sutras* contains seeds that, when contemplated, reveal the essence of many worldviews.

There are varying opinions as to the actual substance of the original manuscript. Some sources claim 194 sutras, others claim 196. Here, I have followed what is generally considered to be the complete text, consisting of 196 aphorisms, separated into four chapters. This arrangement follows an Indian tradition that holds that a scripture should generally contain four parts:

1. a chosen goal
2. the current status of man
3. the path by which the now imperfect man can reach the goal of perfection
4. the man-of-perfection's attitude to the world after achieving his goal[1]

---

[1] Swami Chinmayananda's Introduction, in Swami Nityananda (of Vajreshwari), *Voice of the Self,* Madras, India: Ramanath Pai, publisher, 1962, p. *xix.*

Some scholars argue that the original *Sutra* text had only three chapters, because the third chapter ends with the word *iti,* denoting "the end" or, more literally, "that's all." For some scholars, the arrangement of the *Sutras* is rough.

In the Krishnamacharya tradition, however, the arrangement was intentional, for Patanjali wrote each chapter, not as components of a system, but rather as a personalized teaching for his four principal students. From this perspective, each chapter can be seen as an adaptation for four unique individuals who, in turn, represent the archetypes of yoga students.

The first chapter of the *Yoga Sutras,* Samadhi Pada—On Being Absorbed in Spirit, conveys the depth of the tradition's teachings in fifty-one sutras. It is appropriate for the most advanced students, *kritanjali.* Here, Patanjali details the process of separating your identity from your thoughts, the development of the concentration necessary for absorption into Spirit, and the method for knowing the Lord of All. This chapter reveals concepts elaborated upon in the earlier philosophical system of *samkhya.* Its first three sutras describe the highest state of yoga, *samadhi,* or communion with one's spiritual essence. In the traditional Vedic sutra form of writing, the teachings begin and end with the highest teachings. The most advanced students need nothing more. The remainder of the chapter is merely an explanation of these first three sutras.

This first chapter describes the Lord of All and how that One is to be known. This teaching appears nowhere else in classical yogic teachings. When asked to define the proper object of meditation following a two-week intensive, Krishnamacharya replied, *Isvara-pranidhana,* or surrender to the inner Lord of All. Here the devotional path of Bhakti Yoga is offered to the humble student.

Chapter II, Sadhana Pada—On Practices for Being Immersed in Spirit, contains the practical means to attain the goal set forth in the first chapter. It is the second longest chapter, comprised of fifty-five sutras. According to Krishnamacharya, this section was written for Patanjali's student Baddhanjali. Baddhanjali characterizes the status of the majority of yoga students, whose paths are filled with obstacles and who have impurities within them that must be removed. This chapter is also called *Kriya Yoga*, a method of purifying oneself to attain the awareness necessary for immersion into the Self (or one's chosen deity) to arise naturally. This chapter contains much practical advice on the nature of the mind, the nature and removal of suffering, and how to live a yogic lifestyle. The process incorporates social and person ethical guidelines, so that one can be developed into an ideal personality who seeks to benefit the whole of society.

Chapter II contains the famous eightfold path (*Ashtanga Yoga*), which begins with sutra II, 29 and extends to sutra III, 3. These aphorisms give guidelines for the successful practice of *Hatha Yoga* as a prelude to discipline of the mind through meditational exercises. This is the process known as *Raja Yoga*, whereby your awareness is transformed from an identification with the physical body and mind into a comprehension of hidden, underlying bodies composed of energy and light through the *asana-pranayama-pratyahara* formula (see II, 46–II, 55). The raja yogi seeks nothing less than a complete transformation of Self into a body of light.

Chapter III, Vibhuti Pada—On Supernatural Abilities and Gifts, completes the alchemical transformation formula with aphorisms on the process of *samyama*. This is the longest chapter, containing fifty-six sutras. According to Krishnamacharya, it was written for Patanjali's third student, Mastakanjali who had mastered his physical body and developed his power of concentration sufficiently to begin to unravel mysterious supernatural abilities, revealing the full range of mind and consciousness. Through Patanjali's guidance, students using this chapter can develop a continuous stream of mindfulness (*samyama*) ranging from concentration, to meditation, to absorption of an object's spiritual essence (*dharana-dhyana-samadhi*). Patanjali then explains how this process may be mastered into a contemplative and energetic flow into Spirit itself, giving many examples of how to focus the mind on different objects of meditation. Using these exercises, students may receive supernormal abilities (*siddhis*) as gifts from the Divine Spirit (*vibhuti*). Students are cautioned, however, in sutra III, 38, that these gifts and powers are impediments to the goal of *samadhi* (absorption into the divine spirit). Through the discipline of focusing upon the underlying Divine Spirit that gives all gifts and powers, spiritual seekers (*sadhakas*) gradually free their minds of attachments to the many pleasures and powers of the seen and hidden worlds.

Chapter IV, Kaivalya Pada—On Absolute Freedom, was given to Patanjali's fourth student, Purnanjali. This advanced student merely needed a summary of the tradition's teachings to prepare him for the final step to spiritual integration. Here, Patanjali clarifies the power of the primal forces of nature (*gunas*) and elaborates on how to transcend the limitations of space and time. He makes it clear that yoga's goal is a continually unfolding process of self-knowledge through fulfillment of life's four arenas of activity: *dharma* (righteous duty), *artha* (prosperity), *kama* (sensual pleasure), and *moksha* (spiritual liberation). The goal of this process is no less than freedom from all limitations and attachments through completely integrating yourself as a spiritual and physical being.

RECOMMENDATIONS TO YOGA STUDENTS

This presentation of the *Yoga Sutras* is meant as an aid to contemplation. Through a regular reading of it, you naturally engage in the process of self-reflection (*svadhyaya*)—just as when you are captivated by a beautiful sunset or the fragrance of an aromatic flower, or when you are shocked by the death of a dearly beloved into a naturally arising deep mental concentration. I believe that Patanjali wrote this text with the intention of keeping his readers in a specific mental state conducive to the revelation of their true nature (*purusa*). He meant to show how that nature hides itself, and how, through self-discipline and grace, the innate spiritual essence can unveil itself.

I recommend spending extra time with those aphorisms that resonate for you. On a more practical note, I suggest that you do *yoga sadhana* in the context of Patanjali's guidance. If you are a yoga practitioner and yogasanas and pranayama are the core of your practice, I especially recommend regular reflection upon sutras II, 46 through II, 55. These sutras are powerful tools for transforming the direction of your practice. They are the transitional sutras that allow Hatha Yoga to deepen profoundly, thus becoming Raja Yoga.

The sutras on the process of entering the state of meditation begin after the descriptions of asana-pranayama-pratyahara, sutra III, I. The more specific states of consciousness associated with meditation occur in the beginning of chapter III and are applicable to anyone meditating, regardless of the technique. Thus these sutras provide help for those seeking to focus their minds, regardless of their objectives. They will help religious persons to pray and commune more deeply, and secular people to focus their minds on readily achieving their worldly objectives.

For those seeking the doorway to wisdom and insight, known as Raja Yoga and *Jnana Yoga,* I recommend practice of the meditation techniques cited in sutras I, 33 through 39. Utilizing these six sutras as specific meditation techniques can be of great benefit in your evolution. Each of the practices should be done until you have directly achieved the culmination experiences described in the text. It is important, in this practice, to distinguish between understanding and experience. "Never think that what you understand from scriptures is your own understanding. Never think what you understand from words has become your own experience. Learning is borrowed, wisdom is gained only from direct experience."[2] Remember that practice is a way for your yoga education to provide you with spiritual experiences. Clarity in sharing with others

---

2 Osho, *Enlightenment: the Only Revolution—Discourses on the Great Mystic Ashtavakra.* Pune, India: The Rebel Publishing House, Pvt., Ltd., 1997, p. 203.

is a natural by-product of coming to know the spirit directly. Only from this and your teacher's permission can you transmit something of value.

Yoga Therapy and Ayurveda

For those seeking therapy, the sutras describing the process of yoga therapy and Ayurveda are contained in sutras II, I through 28. The keys to understanding this process are hidden within sutra II, I, which describes the threefold process of *Kriya Yoga* necessary to prepare the mind for the experience of yoga. The process consists of self-study (*svadhyaya*), self-discipline (*tapas*), and devotion to the Lord of Yoga (*Isvarapranidhana*). According to the Ayurvedic perspective, by developing these three qualities the student is also evolving the three primal qualities of biological and psychological functions called the *doshas*. The doshas are fundamental element combinations of ether/air, fire/water, water/earth as they manifest within the visible world. They are respectively called *vata, pitta,* and *kapha.* The yogic practices of self-study evolve the subtle air and ether qualities of vata into *prana* promoting greater intuition. The practice of self-discipline and purification evolve the fire and water of pitta into tejas giving the mind radiant discrimination. Similarly, when devotion to the Lord of Yoga is maintained, it produces humility and awareness of Oneness as *ojas* is created from the more fundamental quality of *kapha's* earth and water.

When studied together, Ayurveda and Classical Yoga have tremendous potential for speeding up the course of one's maturity. As Sri Aurobindo said, "Yoga is condensed evolution." The combination of Ayurvedic guidelines for optimal health and longevity and the spiritual context of Classical Yoga can greatly improve your ability to maintain a balanced perspective in day-to-day life.

Yoga Sutras of Patanjali

CHAPTER I

SAMADHI PADA

On Being Absorbed in Spirit

I, 1

With great respect and love,
now the blessings of
Yoga instruction
are offered.

I, 2

Yoga
is experienced
in that mind
which has
ceased
to identify itself
with its
vacillating waves of perception.

I, 3

When this happens,
then the Seer is revealed,
resting in its own essential nature,
and one realizes
the True
Self.

I, 4

At all other times,
the Self

appears
to assume the form
of thought's
vacillations
and the True Self
is
lost.

I, 5

The vacillations
are of five types,
which may be either
painful
or not painful.

I, 6

The five vacillations are
correct perception,
misconception,
imagination,
sleep,
and memory.

I, 7

The sources of correct understanding are
direct perception,
inference, and
revelation
derived from
reflections on the scriptures,
or from the testimony
of one who knows.

3

I, 8

Misconception is an
illusory knowledge
founded on an unreliable appearance
lacking its own inherent integrity.

I, 9

Imagination is a
fluctuating knowledge
created by relying upon
the sound of language alone,
and words that are
empty of objective truth.

I, 10

Sleep is a
vacillation of understanding
dependent upon the
absence of mindfulness.

I, 11

Memory is a
vacillation of knowledge
created by
not allowing the objects of
sensory experience
to escape.

I, 12

The vacillating waves of perceptions
are stilled through
consistent earnest practice
and
dispassionate non-attachment.

I, 13

Of these two,
practice
is the continuous struggle
to become firmly established
in the stable state
of the True Self.

I, 14

That practice
is indeed firmly grounded
when it is pursued incessantly,
with reverence,
for a long time.

I, 15

Non-attachment
is the mastery of consciousness,
wherein one is free from craving
objects of enjoyment,
whether they have been perceived
or imagined from
promises in scriptures.

I, 16

The ultimate state of non-attachment
arises from self-realization,
in which there is indifference
to the primordial forces of desire, *– guna*
as everything
and everyone
is experienced as one's
own True Self.

I, 17

Thorough knowledge
is accompanied by inquiry
into its four forms
1. analytical thinking about an object,
2. meditative insights on thoughts,
3 reflections into the nature of bliss,
4 and inquiry into one's essential purity.

I, 18

Another form
of thorough knowledge
is preceded by resolute practice
to completely cease
identification with the contents of the mind.
As a result,
only subliminal impressions remain
and their residue
has no impact on the mind.

I, 19

Thorough knowledge
may arise from one's disposition at birth
as in the case of illumined souls
who experience only
their incorporeal state,
merged with nature.

I, 20

For others
who are not born

with this thorough knowledge,
being absorbed in Spirit
is preceded by faith,
indomitable vigor,
and a mindfulness
that is always concerned
with the wisdom
of Oneness.

I, 21

For those who have
an intense urge for Spirit
and wisdom,
it sits near them,
waiting.

I, 22

For those who have an urge of varying degrees—
mild, moderate, or intense—
due to these differences,
there also arise distinctions
in their sense of closeness
to Spirit.

I, 23

The end of spiritual practice
is only attained
by placing oneself
in the Lord.

I, 24

The Lord
is a distinct Self,
untouched
by any form of affliction,
by karma and its effects,
or by the latent impressions
of past actions.

I, 25

In that Self
is the unsurpassed
source of omniscience.

I, 26

That Self
is also unlimited by time,
and is the guru
of the most ancient spiritual teachers.

I, 27

The sound denoting
that Self is
the eternal vibration *Aum*,
which manifests the
grace of the
divine presence.

I, 28

By constantly repeating
that sacred sound

Mukunda Stiles

with great respect and love
and reflecting
upon its meaning,
one attains spiritual wealth.

I, 29

From that practice
arises the attainment of
inward-directed consciousness,
and also
the obstacles
to success
disappear.

depression doubt
laziness craving
disease delusions
poor concentration

I, 30

These obstacles
to self-knowledge
disrupt and scatter the mind—
they are
disease,
dullness,
doubt,
negligence,
laziness,
dissipation resulting from excess craving,
delusion,
lack of achieving the concentration
necessary to achieve
higher consciousness,
and instability.

I, 31

Accompanying
these distractions are
suffering,
frustration,
restlessness,
and disturbed inhalation and exhalation.

I, 32

In order to prevent
these obstacles from arising,
you should habituate
yourself to meditation
upon a
single principle.

I, 33

By cultivating attitudes
of friendliness
toward happiness,
compassion
toward suffering,
delight
toward virtue,
and equanimity
toward vice,
thoughts become purified,
and the obstacles
to self-knowledge
are lessened.

I, 34

Or the obstacles
can be lessened
by forcibly exhaling,
then retaining the prana
during the pause
following the exhalation.

I, 35

Or another way
to steady the mind
is by binding it to
higher, subtler
sense perceptions.

I, 36

Or the mind
can also find peace
by contemplating
the luminous light,
arising from the heart
which is the source of
true serenity.

I, 37

Or another way
is to make the mind's object
a self-realized being
who has transcended
human passions and attachments.

I, 38

Or serenity
can come by
letting the mind be grounded
in knowledge
that has arisen from dreams
or from
the dreamless state of
deep sleep.

I, 39

Or another way
is persistent meditation
in harmony with your
religious heritage.

I, 40

Mastery of tranquillity
extends from the
most minute particle
to the largest,
the form of the entire cosmos.

that's pretty

I, 41

One
whose vacillations
are steadily diminishing
experiences the mind
as transparent,
just as a high-quality gemstone
reveals the form of objects
placed near it.

Mukunda Stiles

They attain
a state of absorption
wherein the knower,
the experience of knowing,
and the object of knowledge
fuse
into one
indistinguishable
subject-object.

I, 42

There is another
state of absorption
in which an object's qualities—
name, meaning, our knowledge of it,
and our assumptions about it
become blended together,
so that thoughtful distinctions
cannot be made.

I, 43

When the
storehouse of memories and impressions
is completely purified,
perception is
empty of vacillations,
and only the object's
true essence
shines forth in
thought-free perception.

I, 44

Specifically by this process
of absorption with reflection
and absorption beyond reflection,
is the perception of
subtle objects is explained.

I, 45

The process of subtle perception
extends to that
which is without form
and is pure consciousness.

I, 46

These absorptions
are also
accompanied by objective goals,
and are called
absorption with seed.

I, 47

From skillfulness in maintaining
an undisturbed flow
of reflection without seed,
arises illumination of the Inner Self.

I, 48

Therein
dwells a luminous wisdom
that upholds the
essence of truth.

Mukunda Stiles

I, 49

From this
luminous wisdom
arise unique insights
distinguished from those gained
from scriptural study or inference,
as they serve
a special purpose.

I, 50

Born of this
luminous wisdom is a
subliminal impression
that prevents other impressions
from arising.

I, 51

When the mind
becomes free from obstruction,
all vacillations cease,
and the mind becomes
absorbed into spirit
without producing future seeds.
Thus a new mind is born
of this wisdom,
free of ignorance.

CHAPTER II

SADHANA PADA

On Practices for Being Immersed in Spirit

II, 1

The practical means
for attaining higher consciousness
consist of three components:
self-discipline and purification,
self-study,
and devotion
to the Lord.

[handwritten margin notes: 1 self discipline, Purification, 2 self study, 3 devotion to the Lord]

II, 2

These practices
cultivate an attitude conducive
to being absorbed in Spirit
and minimize
the power
of the primal causes of suffering.

II, 3

There are five
primal causes of suffering:
ignorance
of your True Self
and the value of spirituality;
egoism
and its self-centeredness;

16

attachment
to pleasure;
aversion
to pain;
and clinging to life
out of fear of death.

II, 4

Ignorance
is the fertile soil,
and, as a
consequence,
all other
obstacles persist.
They may exist in any state—
dormant,
feeble,
intermittent,
or fully operative.

II, 5

Ignorance
is the view
that the ephemeral,
the impure,
the pain of suffering
—that which is not the Self—
is permanent,
pure,
pleasurable,
and the True Self.

II, 6

Egoism is the
enmeshing function of the
mind as an instrument
of perception,
as if it were
the Seer's
power of consciousness.

II, 7

Attachment
is the dwelling upon
pleasure.

II, 8

Aversion
is the dwelling upon
pain.

II, 9

Clinging to life
and the fear of death
are sustained by an intrinsic force
in the same way
that the other primal causes of suffering persist
dominating even the wise.

II, 10

When these
primal causes of suffering
exist in a subtle yet potential form,
they are to be reduced, then destroyed

by the process of involution,
returning them to their source,
the True Self.

II, 11

Their variations
are reduced or overcome
through
meditation.

II, 12

The reservoir of subliminal impressions
is the root of the
primal causes of suffering,
producing obstacles and experiences
both in the present
and in unforeseeable
future lives.

II, 13

As long as this
karmic root exists,
the obstacles continue to mature,
predetermining one's
social status, life-span, and experiences.

II, 14

These results may be
joyous or sorrowful,
depending upon one's
accumulated
merit or demerit.

II, 15

To the discriminating person,
all actions result in only pain.
This pain can arise as a
direct consequence of an action,
in the form of
anguish from unfulfilled desires
and torment from the unwanted
or as a subliminal impression.
Pain can also arise as
a conflict
between thought's vacillations
and the primal
natural forces of desire.

II, 16

The suffering from
pain that has
not yet arisen
is
avoidable.

II, 17

The cause of that
avoidable pain
is the illusory union
of the Seer with the seen,
so that one does not possess
discriminative knowledge of
the True Self.

II, 18

The seen has the qualities of
luminosity, activity, and stability.
It is embodied through the elements
and the sense organs.
It exists
for the dual purpose of
sensory enjoyment
and liberation
of the Self.

II, 19

The stages of manifestation
of the primal forces of desire are fourfold:
specific differentiation of subject and object,
nonspecific fusing of subject and object,
with form, an awareness of an object's essence,
and without form, a state of superconsciousness.

II, 20

The Seer is
pure consciousness only.
Even though
it appears to see
by directing thoughts and concepts,
it remains unchanged
by the mind's operations.

II, 21

For the sake
of that Self alone
does the seen world exist.

II, 22

Those who know the True Self
have fulfilled life's purpose.
For them, the seen world
ceases to exist,
although, to others
who share the common mind,
it does exist.

II, 23

The association
of the Owner
with its possessions
is for the purpose of obtaining
the power of both
and, through discrimination,
realizing one's
essential nature.

II, 24

Ignorance
of the True Self
is the cause of this illusory union.

II, 25

By the elimination
of that ignorance,
the illusory union
also disappears.
This is the remedy
for the Seer's
absolute freedom.

II, 26

The means for this remedy is
the cultivation of unbroken
discriminative awareness.

II, 27

Through this process,
wisdom progresses through
seven phases,
until it extends to
its fullest realm.

II, 28

By sustained practice
of all the component parts of yoga,
the impurities dwindle away
and wisdom's radiant light
shines forth
with discriminative knowledge.

II, 29

Yoga's eight component parts
are self-control
for social harmony,
precepts
for personal discipline,
yoga pose,
regulation of prana,
withdrawal of the senses from their objects,
contemplation of our true nature,
meditation on the True Self,
and being absorbed in Spirit.

II, 30

Self-control
consists of five principles:
non-violence,
truthfulness,
freedom from stealing,
behavior that respects
the Divine as omnipresent,
and freedom from greed.

II, 31

These are called the
great universal vows
when they are extended unconditionally
to nurture everyone,
regardless of status,
place, time, or circumstance.

II, 32

The precepts also *personal discipline*
consist of five principles:
purity,
contentment,
self-discipline and purification,
self-study,
and devotion
to the Lord of Yoga.

II, 33

When you are disturbed
by unwholesome
negative thoughts or emotions,
cultivation of their opposites

promotes self-control
and firmness
in the precepts.

II, 34

Negative thoughts and emotions
are violent,
in that they cause injury
to yourself and others,
regardless of whether
they are performed
by you,
done by others,
or you permit them to be done.
They arise from greed,
anger, or delusion
regardless of whether they
arise from mild,
moderate, or excessive
emotional intensity.
They result in
endless misery and ignorance.
Therefore, when you consistently cultivate
the opposite thoughts and emotions,
the unwholesome tendencies
are gradually destroyed.

II, 35

By abiding
in nonviolence,
one's presence
creates an atmosphere
in which hostility ceases.

II, 36

By abiding
in truthfulness,
one's words and actions
are subservient to truth
and thus whatever is said or done
bears the fruit of that sincerity.

II, 37

By abiding
in freedom from the desire
for other's possessions,
that which is precious
is revealed,
and all that is beneficial
is freely given.

II, 38

By abiding
in behavior that respects
the Divine as omnipresent,
one acquires
an inspired passion for life.

II, 39

Upon the foundation
of freedom from greed,
one gains insight
into the reasons
for the cycles of
birth and death.

II, 40

From purity arises
a desire to protect
one's body
and a cessation of adverse
contact with others.

II, 41

From the purification
of one's essence
cheerfulness arises,
and with it,
one-pointed concentration,
mastery of the senses,
and the capacity
for sustaining
the vision of
the True Self.

II, 42

From contentment
one gains
supreme happiness.

II, 43

Through the intensity of
self-discipline and purification
comes the dwindling
of all impurities
and the perfection
of the body
and senses.

II, 44

From self-study
comes communion
with one's
chosen personal deity.

II, 45

From devotion
to the Lord,
one is given perfect
absorption into Spirit.

II, 46

Yoga pose
is a steady
and comfortable position.

II, 47

Yoga pose is mastered
by relaxation of effort,
lessening the tendency
for restless breathing,
and promoting an identification
of oneself as living
within
the infinite breath of life.

II, 48

From that
perfection of yoga posture,
duality,

such as reacting to praise and criticism,
ceases
to be a disturbance.

II, 49

When this is acquired,
pranayama naturally follows,
with a cessation
of the movements
of inspiration and expiration.

II, 50

The vacillations of prana
are either external,
internal, or stationary.
They may be regulated in
three ways:
by location, time, or number;
then they will become
prolonged and subtle.

II, 51

In the fourth method
of regulating one's breath, prana
is extended
into the divine life force
and the range of prana
is felt permeating everywhere,
transcending the attention
given to either
external or internal objects.

II, 52

As a result
of this pranayama,
the veil obscuring the radiant
supreme light of the Inner Self
dissolves.

II, 53

And as a result,
the mind attains fitness
for the process of contemplation
of the True Self.

II, 54

When the energy of the senses withdraws
and the impetus
to come into contact
with their objects ceases,
the senses imitate,
as it were,
the essential nature
of pure consciousness.

II, 55

From that arises
the highest mastery
over the senses.

CHAPTER III

VIBHUTI PADA

On Supernatural Abilities and Gifts

III, I

Contemplation
is
the confining
of thought
to one point.

III, 2

Meditation
depends upon this
foundation for directing thoughts
into a continuous flow
of awareness.

III, 3

Being absorbed in Spirit
is that consciousness,
whose object is
void of form or goal
and only the
essence of the object
remains
shining forth.

III, 4

Samyama
occurs when these three processes
flow together harmoniously,
integrating the full spectrum
of the mind's potential.

III, 5

By mastering this,
the light of
transcendental insight
dawns.

III, 6

Its progression
is in stages,
ranging from meditations on
gross material objects
to gradually subtler regions.

III, 7

These three
constitute
the internal portions
of yoga,
in contrast
to the previous
five external portions.

III, 8

Even these three
are external

to the innermost part:
being absorbed in Spirit
without seed,
without attachment
to an outcome.

III, 9

From this,
there is a true
transformation of the mind
as outgoing thoughts cease
their former pattern of reacting
to the appearance or disappearance
of subliminal impressions.
Instead, moments of restrained thought
predominate.

III, 10

By frequent repetition
of that restraint
an undisturbed flow
of tranquillity results.

III, 11

In the process of
being absorbed in Spirit,
the thought process experiences
a second transformation
resulting from the continuous
appearance of one-pointedness
and the disappearance of distraction.

III, 12

Then again,
a third transformation occurs
from the one-pointedness that results
as the
rising and subsiding
thoughts
become equal.

III, 13

By these three processes,
there is a transformation of the mind's
quality, character, and condition.
In the same manner,
there is a spiritual transformation
of the senses,
and even in one's constitutional elements.

III, 14

Our nature has
a common source—
the substratum out of which all
latent, manifest,
and unmanifested properties
of consciousness arise.

III, 15

Variations in
sequential progression
are the cause of apparent differences
in spiritual transformation.

Mukunda Stiles

III, 16

By the practice of samyama
on the preceding
three transformations of thought—
restraint,
decaying of distractions,
and the balanced state—
one is given knowledge of
the past and future.

III, 17

Confusion arises upon the
superimposition of a word,
its meaning,
and one's ideas about it.
By practicing samyama
on these distinctions
with a resolve for clarity,
one is given
knowledge of the speech
of all living beings.

III, 18

By direct perception
of residual
subliminal impressions,
one is blessed with
knowledge of
previous births.

III, 19

By insight
into another's perceptions
one is blessed with the
knowledge of
their point of view.

III, 20

But the ability
to read another's mind is
not gained with the support
of this perception,
as specific thoughts are not
the object of samyama.

III, 21

By the practice of samyama
on the form of your body,
you disappear,
as you suspend
the receptive power of light
from being received
by others' eyes.

III, 22

By this samyama process applied
to sound and the other senses,
the disappearance of
sensory perceptions
has been described.

III, 23

Karma has two aspects:
actions whose results are occurring,
and actions whose fruit is yet to come.
By the practice of samyama on karma,
one gains knowledge
of the proximity of death,
or this insight can come
from subtle physical signs.

III, 24

By the practice of samyama
on friendliness and other virtues,
one gains their full power.

III, 25

By the practice of samyama
on the strength of an elephant
and the virtues of
other animals,
one gains corresponding strengths
and other virtues.

III, 26

Knowledge of subtle, obscure,
and remote objects is given
by projecting onto them
the brilliance of
the mind's power of
supersensory perception.

III, 27

By the practice of samyama
on the Sun,
knowledge of the solar system
and other planes of existence
is given.

III, 28

By the practice of samyama
on the Moon,
knowledge of the organization
of the stars
is given.

III, 29

By the practice of samyama on the Pole Star,
from that contemplation
knowledge of stellar movements
is given.

III, 30

By the practice of samyama
on the navel's psychic center,
knowledge
of the organization and functions
of the body
arises.

III, 31

By the practice of samyama
on the cavity
of the throat,
hunger and thirst
cease.

III, 32

By the practice of samyama
on the tortoise-shaped
subtle channel
below the throat's cavity,
motionlessness
is gained.

III, 33

By the practice of samyama
on the light
in the crown of the head,
a spiritual vision
bestowing the blessings
of perfected masters
is given.

III, 34

Or all knowledge
can be given through
a flash of intuitive illumination.

III, 35

By the practice of samyama
on the spiritual heart,
complete knowledge
of the mind,
its vacillations,
and the whole range
of one's thought
is given.

III, 36

The lucid mind and
the Transcendental Self
are absolutely distinct.
The mind directs awareness
for the sake of
sensual experiences.
The Self exists for its own sake
and remains separate.
Without distinguishing this difference,
worldly experience happens.
By the practice of samyama
on this distinction,
knowledge of the Self
is gained.

III, 37

From this discrimination
spiritual perceptions
are born in all the senses:
flashes of intuition illuminate
the past, future,
and things hidden;
divine sounds
emanate from within;
divine touch
permeates the body;
divine vision
reveals the Divine
as the world;
divine taste
secretes ambrosial nectar

into the mouth;
and a divine fragrance
emanates an intoxicating aroma.

III, 38

These gifts
are impediments
to being absorbed in Spirit,
but they are seen
as the attainment of perfection
to the
worldly minded.

III, 39

By loosening
the causes of bondage
and becoming sensitive
to the nuances of psychic pathways,
one's perceptions can enter another's
body.

III, 40

By mastery *contracted in the throat and moved upward*
of udana prana,
which moves up from the chest,
one can encounter obstacles
like water, mud, thorns, and so on
without contacting them
and, through this pranic current,
ascend
from gravity.

III, 41

By mastery
of samana prana
circulating outward from the abdomen,
one appears to radiate light.

III, 42

By the practice of samyama
on the interrelationship of
hearing and the element of ether as space,
one experiences the omnipresence of divine hearing.

III, 43

By the practice of samyama
on the relationship between
the body and the element of ether as space,
and by becoming one with
the lightness of cotton,
one's consciousness can move
through space
anywhere.

III, 44

During this great out-of-body experience,
the mind's vacillations
seem unimaginable,
as they are perceived
to be external to oneself,
and, from this experience,
the covering
hiding spiritual illumination
begins to disperse.

III, 45

By the practice of samyama
on the various states
of the elements—
gross, intrinsic,
subtle, all pervasive—
and seeking to know their
abundant purposes,
one gains
mastery over the elements.

III, 46

From this arises
attainments,
like becoming minute,
creating a sense of wealth
from the perfection
of one's attributes.
Then the body is
not an obstruction
on the journey
to self-realization.

III, 47

The wealth of perfections
thus acquired include
beauty, gracefulness,
strength, and the
extraordinary durability
of a diamond.

III, 48

By the practice of samyama
on the functions and
purposes of the senses—
directing perception,
their essential nature,
exploring all pervasiveness
and remaining indifferent—
one gains
mastery of the senses.

III, 49

From this,
the senses move with the
swiftness of thought
as they become
independent of their sensory organs,
and there is mastery over
the primal cause of matter.

III, 50

Only from the knowledge
of the distinction
between purity of mind
and identification with the True Self
comes omniscience and supremacy
over all states and manifestations
of the mind.

III,51

By nonattachment
even to that
comes the dwindling

of the seeds of bondage
and absolute freedom
is experienced.

III, 52

Even when the highest celestial beings
admire you,
you should once again avoid
attachment
and the resulting pride,
because of the potential for the
revival of the
undesirable.

III, 53

By the practice of samyama
on the moments of time
and its orderly succession
one gains knowledge
born of discrimination.

III, 54

From this,
one gains
an understanding
that clarifies
the differences
between two similar objects
that are otherwise indistinguishable
by their origin,
distinctive characteristics,
or position.

III, 55

Thus,
knowledge
born of discrimination
is the liberator
unto absolute freedom;
it recognizes all objects
in all conditions,
regardless of their
sequential appearance.

III, 56

Therefore,
when the purified mind
becomes equal in purity
with the Transcendental Self,
then
absolute freedom
arises.

CHAPTER IV

KAIVALYA PADA

On Absolute Freedom

IV, 1

Supernatural powers
can result from
an exalted birth,
magical herbs,
mantras,
intense spiritual practice,
or absorption into Spirit.

IV, 2

By living in the abundance
of nature's
overflowing creativity,
you may be transformed
and elevated
from your perspective
achieved during previous births.

IV, 3

These incidental causes are an
indirect means to spiritual evolution,
as they are naturally arising.
On the other hand,
they are like the farmer
who removes barriers
to allow water to flow
for the flowering
of the field.

IV, 4

Solely from the
sense of individuality
are mental fabrications
produced.

IV, 5

There is a multiplicity
of activities of the mind,
yet one thought
is the originator
of the diversity
of thoughts.

IV, 6

Of these thoughts,
the one
born of meditation
is free
from accumulating
karmic impressions
that create further
ignorance and attachment.

IV, 7

The actions of such a yogi
are neither white nor black;
for others,
their actions are threefold,
white, black, and mixed.

IV, 8

From the maturation
of these residual impressions,
only corresponding
potential desires
manifest.

IV, 9

Because residual
impressions
and memory are identical,
their continuity is sustained,
although they may appear
to be separated by differences
in birth,
place, or time.

IV, 10

There is
no beginning
to this cycle,
and,
because of the permanence
of the primal will to live,
there is no end.

IV, 11

Cause and effect,
support and its supported object
are inseparable,
in the same manner, so are impressions
and memory bound together.
With the absence
of one of these factors,
impressions will
vanish.

IV, 12

The past and future exist
in their own essential form.
Yet, owing to differences
in characteristics,
they manifest
at their own pace.

IV, 13

These characteristics,
manifest or unmanifested,
are due to
primal natural forces.

IV, 14

Modification of characteristics
occurs through this process,
yet
the essence of the object
remains constant
due to the oneness
of life.

IV, 15

Though the essence of
objects remains the same,
owing to differences
in the mind,
people have distinct perceptions
of the same object.

IV, 16

And,
if an object
dependant upon one mind
were not recognized
by that mind,
what then
would exist?

IV, 17

The mind
depends upon its
coloring an object;
by that is the object
known
or unknown.

IV, 18

The vacillations of thought
are always known
to its master,
the True Self,
due to its
constancy.

IV, 19

Thought is an object
and therefore
cannot
illuminate itself.

IV, 20

And there can be no
comprehension of
both subject and object
simultaneously.

IV, 21

If it were possible
to know another's thoughts,
every mind could know
every other's thoughts
and the result
would be a
confusion of impressions,
which would be
an impossible absurdity.

IV, 22

An evolved consciousness
experiences one's own Self
by the reflection of the
changeless Self
arising as the
field of consciousness.
In that form,
the Self
is known.

Mukunda Stiles

IV, 23

The conscious mind
can comprehend everything,
as it is colored
by the reflections of the
Seer and the seen.

IV, 24

The mind accumulates
countless desires,
although
it exists solely
for the sake
of being close
to the True Self.

IV, 25

Dwelling upon
self-centeredness
completely ceases
for one who sees
this distinction.

IV, 26

Then the mind
is inclined
toward discriminative thinking,
which pulls irresistibly
toward
absolute freedom.

IV, 27

In the intervals between
these discriminative thoughts,
distracting thoughts
arise
due to other past
habitual thoughts.

IV, 28

Their cessation
is like that of the obstacles
that were previously
described,
that is, destroying them
through meditative absorption.

IV, 29

One who is free of self-interest,
even from the attainment of
the highest realizations,
and who possesses
constant discrimination
is showered with virtues
from being
absorbed in Spirit.

IV, 30

From this
comes a
cessation of obstacles
and
karmic patterns.

IV, 31

Then all the
obscuring veils
and impurities are removed
due to the endlessness
of self-knowledge.
Then only trivial knowledge
of the objective world
remains hidden.

IV, 32

Thereafter,
having fulfilled their purpose
through the
series of transformations,
the power of the
primal natural forces
terminates.

IV, 33

As these forces
come to an end,
time is slowed
to such a degree
that the moments
that correspond to
the sequence of
these transformations
become readily comprehended.

IV, 34

Absolute freedom results
when the primal natural forces,
having no further purpose to serve,
become re-absorbed
to the source of all,
or
when the power of pure consciousness
becomes established in its
own essential nature.

THE END.

↩ *Mukunda Stiles*

Summary of Patanjali's Yoga Sutras

CHAPTER I

SAMADHI PADA

On Being Absorbed in Spirit

CHAPTER II

SADHANA PADA

On Practices for Being Immersed in Spirit

VIBHUTI PADA

On Supernatural Abilities and Gifts

CHAPTER IV

KAIVALYA PADA

On Absolute Freedom

Sanskrit Text
with Word-by-Word Translation

SAMADHI PADA

On Being Absorbed in Spirit

I, 1
atha yoganusasanam

atha—now

yoga—yoga

anusasanam—instruction, orderly arrangement

I, 2
yogah citta vrtti nirodhah

yogah—yoga

citta—thought, mind, perception (*cit* = to perceive, be bright)

vrtti—vacillation, turning, twist (*vrt* = to whirl)

nirodhah—cease, stop, completely contained (*ni* = to negate + *rodha* from Rudra, the god/goddess of storms)

I, 3
tada drastuh svarupe avasthanam

tada—then, at that time

drastuh—Seer

svarupe—in one's own form, essence, essential nature

avasthanam—abides, rests (*ava* + *stha* = to stand)

I, 4
vrtti sarupyam itaratra

vrtti—vacillation, turning, twist (*vrt* = to whirl)

sarupyam—conformity, identification, assumes the form

itaratra—elsewhere, at other times, otherwise

I, 5

vrttayah pancatayyah klista aklistah

vrttayah—(plural of *vrtti*) vacillation, turning, twist (*vrt* = to whirl)
pancatayyah—fivefold, five types
klista—troublesome, difficult, painful (*klis* = to trouble)
aklistah—not troublesome, non-obstructing, not painful

I, 6

pramana viparyaya vikalpa nidra smrtayah

pramana—right knowledge, correct understanding
viparyaya—misconception, wrong knowledge
vikalpa—imagination, conceptualization
nidra—sleep without content
smrtayah—memory (plural, as it comprises the whole five *vrtteh*)

I, 7

pratyaksa anumana agamah pramanani

pratyaksa—direct perception, sense evidence
anumana—inference
agamah—testimony from an authority, scriptural truths, revelations
pramanani—right knowledge, correct understanding

I, 8

viparyayo mithyajnanam atadrupa pratistham

viparyayo—wrong knowledge, misconception
mithya—erroneous, illusory
jnanam—knowledge
a tad—not that, not its own, its inherent
rupa—appearance, form
pratistham—founded on, based on, steadfast (*pra* = bring forth +
    stha = to stand)

I, 9

sabda jnana anupati vastusunya vikalpah

sabda—sound, word, language

jnana—knowledge

anupati—followed in sequence, relying upon

vastusunya—empty of substance, devoid of meaning

vikalpah—imagination, conceptualization

I, 10

abhava pratyaya alambana vrttih nidra

abhava—absence of awareness, lack of mindfulness

pratyaya—directed awareness, going with conviction

alambana—depending upon, support, depending on a prop

vrttih—vacillation, turning, twist (*vrt* = to whirl)

nidra—sleep without activity

I, 11

anubhuta visaya sampramosah smrtih

anubhuta—experienced, perceived

visaya—objects

asampramosah—non-escaping, not letting go, not allowing to release

smrtih—recollection, memory

I, 12

abhyasa vairagyabhyam tan-nirodhah

abhyasa—repeated practice, uninterrupted vigilance, consistent, earnest practice

vairagyabhyam—dispassionate non-attachment, freedom from desires

tan—that, here, they

nirodhah—suppression, stillness, stop, cease, completely contained

I, 13

tatra sthitau yatnah abhyasah

tatra—there, of these, therein, in that case

sthitau—steadiness, being established, perfect restraint

yatnah—vigilant effort, continuous struggle, exertion

abhyasah—repeated practice, consistent, earnest effort

I, 14

sa tu dirgha kala nairantarya satkara asevitah drdha bhumih

sa—that, this (practice)

tu—moreover, indeed, and

dirgha—long

kala—time

nairantarya—incessantly, without interruption, continuous

satkara—reverent devotion, dedication, sincerity, properly

asevitah—pursued, cultivated, well-tended, zealously practiced

drdha—firm, well-fixed, established

bhumih—ground, firmly rooted (*bhu* = to become)

I, 15

drsta anusravika visaya vitrsnasya vasikara samjna vairagyam

drsta—seen, perceptible, experienced

anusravika—promised in the scriptures or in tradition

visaya—objects, enjoyments

vitrsnasya—without thirst, free from craving, one who is
    free from desire

vasikara—mastery, supremacy, subjugation, under control

samjna—consciousness, full knowledge

vairagyam—lack of desire, dispassion, non-attachment

I, 16

tatparam purusa khyateh guna vaitrsnyam

tat—that, here, this (non-attachment)

param—highest, ultimate, supreme

purusa—True Self

khyateh—due to the realization, identity, knowledge

guna—primary forces of nature, primal desire (*guna* = strand)

vaitrsnyam—lack of desire, indifference

I, 17

vitarka vichara ananda asmita rupa anugamat samprajnatah

vitarka—analytical thinking, logical reasoning

vichara—meditative insight, philosophical reflection

ananda—bliss, joy, elation

asmita —sense of pure being, essential purity

rupa—form, appearance

anugamat—accompanied with, followed by

samprajnatah—samadhi with seed, thorough knowledge

I, 18

virama pratyaya abhyasa purvah samskara sesah anyah

virama—complete cessation, repose, pause, rest

pratyaya—contents of the mind

abhyasa—practice with firm conviction, resolution

purvah—preceded by, coming before

samskara—subliminal impressions

sesah—remainder, residue (*sis* = to remain)

anyah—the other, another, different (samadhi without seed)

I, 19

bhava pratyaya videha prakrtilayanam

bhava—one's disposition at birth

pratyaya—arising from, going toward, causation

videha—disembodied, incorporeal

prakrtilayanam—merged, absorbed in primal nature (feminine),
    primary matter

I, 20

sraddha virya smrti samadhi prajna purvakah itaresam

sraddha—faith

virya—indomitable vigor, valor (*vi* = to approach eagerly)

smrti—mindful, unobstructed memory

samadhi—spiritual absorption, oneness

prajna—higher knowledge, wisdom

purvakah—preceded by, prior

itaresam—for others, whereas another

I, 21

tivra samveganam asannah

tivra—intense, acute

samveganam—for those whose urge is

asannah—sitting near, drawn near, immanent

I, 22

mrdu madhya adhimatra tvat tatah api visesah

mrdu—mild

madhya—moderate

adhimatra—intense, extreme

tvat—due to

tatah—from it, therefore

api—also

visesah—difference, distinction

I, 23

Isvara pranidhanat va

Isvara—Lord (*Is* = to be master of, to reign)

pranidhanat—surrender, devotion, dedication, feeling the
    omnipresence of, placing oneself in

va—only, most important

I, 24

klesa karma vipaka asayaih aparamrstah
purusa visesah Isvarah

klesa—affliction, troublesome, pain, corruption

karma—action

vipaka—result, effects, ripening

asayaih—reservoir of subliminal desires and intentions, latent
impressions of past actions

aparamrstah—unaffected, untouched

purusa—True Self

visesah—special being, distinct, extraordinary

Isvarah—Lord (*Is* = to be master of, to reign)

I, 25

tatra niratisayam sarvajna bijam

tatra—there (in *Isvara*), in that

niratisayam—unsurpassed, unrivaled, the highest, incomparable

sarvajna—omniscient

bijam—seed, source, origin

I, 26

sa purvesam api guruh kalena anavacchedat

sa—that

purvesam—of those who came before, of the ancients

api—also, even

guruh—teacher, master mentor (*gu* + *ru* = darkness to light)

kalena—by time, temporal

anavacchedat—unlimited, unconditioned

I, 27

tasya vacakah pranavah

tasya—of it, of that

vacakah—sound symbol, signifying, expression (*vac* = to speak)

pranavah—*aum*, continuous reverberation, the highest praise
  (*pra* + *na* = to exalt, glorify, shout; *vah* = air)

I, 28

tat japah tad artha bhavanam

tat—that
japah—repetition, mental reflection of mantra
tad—its
artha—meaning, purpose, wealth (*arth* = to intend)
bhavanam—realizing, reflecting upon with the proper attitude

I, 29

tatah pratyak cetana adhigamah api antaraya abhava ca

tatah—from that, then
pratyak—inward, introspection, in the opposite direction
cetana—consciousness
adhigamah—attainment, accomplish, discover
api—also
antaraya—obstacle
abhava—absence, disappearance
ca—and

I, 30

vyadhi styana samsaya pramada alasya avirati bhrantidarsana
alabdha-bhumikatva anavasthitatva
citta viksepah te antarayah

vyadhi—disease
styana—dullness, apathy, lack of interest
samsaya—doubt, indecision
pramada—negligence, inattentiveness, carelessness
alasya—laziness, lethargy (*a* + *las* = not to shine)
avirati—lack of self control, dissipation due to excess sensuality
bhrantidarsana—misconception, delusion, false visions

71

alabdha-bhumikatva—lack of concentration to achieve higher
consciousness
anavasthitatva—instability, inability to retain what is achieved
citta—mind, thought
viksepah—disruption, scattered
te—these, they
antarayah—blocks, obstacles

I, 31

**duhkha daurmanasya angamejayatva svasa prasvasa
viksepa sahbhuvah**

duhkha—distress, pain, grief, unhappiness, suffering
daurmanasya—depression, despair, frustration
angamejayatva—trembling, restlessness
svasa—disturbed inhalation
prasvasa—irregular exhalation
viksepa—distraction, disruption
sahabhuvah—accompanying symptoms, companions

I, 32

tat pratisedha artham eka tattva abhyasah

tat—that, of those
pratisedha—prevention, removal
artham—purpose, in order to
eka—one, single
tattva—principle, truth
abhyasah—practice, habituation

I, 33

**maitri karuna mudita upeksanam sukha duhkha punya apunya
visayanam bhavanatah citta prasadanam**

maitri—friendliness
karuna—compassion, mercy

mudita—gladness, delight, joy

upeksanam—indifference, equanimity, impartiality

sukha—easy, happiness, pleasure

duhkha—pain, sorrow, unhappy, suffering

punya—virtue, meritorious

apunya—evil, vicious, mean, unlawful

visayanam—of the objects, concerning something

bhavanatah—by cultivating attitudes, by constant reflection

citta—mind, thought

prasadanam—purification, undisturbed calmness

I, 34

pracchardana vidharanabhyam va pranasya

pracchardana—forceful expiration (*pra* = to bring forth + *chrid* = to
   expel, vomit)

vidharanabhyam—retention, restraining

va—or

pranasya—of breath, life-force (*pra* = to bring forth + *an* = to breathe)

I, 35

visayavati va pravrttih utpanna
manasah sthiti nibandhani

visayavati—sensuous, sense perception

va—or

pravrttih—higher activity, functioning

utpanna—arisen, brought about

manasah—mental control, of the mind

sthiti—steadiness

nibandhani—holding, fixing, binding

I, 36

visoka va jyotismati

visoka—without sorrow, serenity, transcendental nature

73

va —or

jyotismati—the supreme light, luminous, shining

I, 37

vita raga visayam va cittam

vita—transcend, free from

raga—attachment, passion, desire

visayam—object

va—or

cittam—mind, thought

I, 38

svapna nidra jnana alambanam va

svapna—dream state

nidra—sleep

jnana—knowledge

alambanam—support, dependent upon, grounded, foundation

va—or

I, 39

yatha abhimata dhyanat va

yatha—as, whatever, in accord, in harmony

abhimata—desired, predilection to one's religious heritage

dhyanat—by meditation

va—or

I, 40

parama anu parama mahattva antah asya vasikarah

parama—most

anu—minute, smallest particle, microcosm

parama—most

mahattva—largest, vast, macrocosm

antah—extending, ending, expanse

asya—of his, of this

vasikarah—mastery

I, 41

ksina vrtteh abhijatasya iva maneh grahitri grahana
grahyesu tatstha tadanjanata samapattih

ksina—diminished, dissolving

vrtteh—vacillation, turning, twist (*vrt* = to whirl)

abhijatasya—faultless, purified, beautiful, transparent

iva—like, just as

maneh—of a gemstone, jewel

grahitri—knower, perceiver

grahana—experience, knowable

grahyesu—in what is experienced, to be known

tatstha—on which it rests, remaining stable

tadanjanata—the power to appear in the shape of another object

samapattih—complete identification, fusion

I, 42

tatra sabda artha jnana vikalpaih sankirna
savitarka samapattih

tatra—there

sabda—word, sound, name

artha—true meaning, wealth

jnana—knowledge, ordinary thinking

vikalpaih—imaginary thinking, assumption

sankirna—mixed, blended together, confused

savitarka—thoughtful, with deliberation

samapattih—complete identification, fusion

I, 43

smrti parisuddhau svarupa sunya iva artha matra
nirbhasa nirvitarka

smrti—storehouse of impressions, memory

parisuddhau—completely cleansed, purified

svarupa—own form, essential nature

sunya—devoid, empty

iva—as if

artha—real meaning, wealth

matra—only, alone

nirbhasa—shining, appearing clearly

nirvitarka—without thinking, beyond thought

I, 44

etayaiva savichara nirvichara ca suksma visaya vyakhyata

etayaiva—by this alone, in this way specifically

savichara—absorption with reflection

nirvichara—beyond reflection

ca—and

suksma—subtle

visaya—objects

vyakhyata—explained, described

I, 45

suksma visayatvam ca alinga paryavasanam

suksma—subtle

visayatvam—stages of samadhi, process of perception

ca—and

alinga —unmanifested, without form

paryavasanam—terminates, extending to

I, 46

ta eva sabijah samadhih

ta—those, these

eva—only, also

sabijah—with seed, having an object

samadhih—absorption

I, 47

nirvicara vaisaradye adhyatma prasadah

nirvicara—beyond reflective, reflection without seeds

vaisaradye—on attaining the utmost purity, an undisturbed pure
flow

adhyatma—Inner Self, spiritual Self

prasadah—clarity, illumination, brightness

I, 48

rtam bhara tatra prajna

rtam—truth, essence

bhara—bearing, upholding

tatra—there, in that

prajna—wisdom, insight

I, 49

sruta anumana prajnabhyam anyavisaya visesa arthatvat

sruta—heard based on tradition, scripture

anumana—based on inference, conjecture

prajnabhyam—from the wisdom of insight, from these two means

anyavisaya—another object

visesa—distinction, special, unique

arthatvat—purpose, aim

I, 50

tajjah samskaro anya samskara pratibandhi

tajjah—born of that (knowledge that upholds truth)

samskaro—subliminal impressions

anya—other

samskara—impressions

pratibandhi—prevents, obstructs, contradicts

I, 51

tasyapi nirodhe sarva nirodhat nirbijah samadhih

tasyapi—even of this, of that also

nirodhe—the restriction, cessation, destroying, inhibition, free
from obstruction

sarva—all

nirodhat—owing to the ending, cease

nirbijah—without seed

samadhih—spiritual absorption, merging of subject and object

CHAPTER II

SADHANA PADA

On Practices for Being Immersed in Spirit

II, I

tapah svadhyaya Isvara-pranidhanani kriya yoga

tapah—(*tap* = to heat intensively) self-discipline and purification, austerity, action without desire

svadhyaya—(*sva* = one's own, Self + *dhyaya* = analysis) self- study,
study of spiritual texts and sacred lore

Isvara-pranidhanani—(*Is* = Lord + *svas* = breathe, inhale + *ra* = fire,
to quicken, attitude of attraction and love; *pra* = fullness +
ni = under + *dhana* = placement) surrender to the Lord, place
oneself under the fullness of the Divine

kriya yoga—practical means for attaining higher concentration,
process of purification

II, 2

samadhi bhavana arthah klesa tanu karanarthah ca

samadhi—spiritual absorption, merging of subject and object
bhavana—attitude conducive for, contemplation with feeling
arthah—purpose
klesa—primal causes of suffering, obstacles, afflictions
tanu—minimize, weaken, reduce
karanarthah—for the purpose of causing, for making
ca—and

II, 3

avidya asmita raga dvesa abhinivesah klesah

avidya—ignorance, illusion, lack of knowledge and the value of
spirituality
asmita—egoism, sense of individuality

79

raga—attraction, attachment, desire, passion

dvesa—(*dva* = divide + *sha* = life; to divide life) aversion, dislike, hatred, repulsion

abhinivesah—(*abhi* = moving toward + *ni* = liking + *esha* = life; the movement toward liking life) clinging to life, fear of death

klesah—primal causes of suffering, obstacle, affliction

II, 4

avidya ksetram uttaresam prasupta tanu vicchinna udaranam

avidya—ignorance, illusion, lack of appreciation for spirituality

ksetram—fertile soil, field, source

uttaresam—consequently, that which follows

prasupta—dormant, sleeping

tanu—feeble, attenuated, thin

vicchinna—scattered, hidden, interrupted, intermittent

udaranam—expanded, fully operative, sustained, active

II, 5

anitya asuci duhkha anatmasu nitya suci sukha atma khyatih avidya

anitya—ephemeral, non-eternal

asuci—impure

duhkha—pain, misery, sorrow, suffering

anatmasu—not the Self

nitya—eternal, permanent

suci—pure

sukha—happiness, comfort, pleasure

atma—Self

khyatih—identification, view, opinion

avidya—ignorance, illusion, lack of appreciation for spirituality

II, 6

drg darsana saktyoh ekatmataiva asmita

drg—Seer, power of consciousness/vision

darsana—seeing, perceiving, vision

saktyoh—power, capability of the two

ekatmataiva—identity (one-self-ness), as if it were

asmita—egoism, I-am-ness

II, 7

sukha anusayi ragah

sukha—pleasure, happiness

anusayi—dwells upon, accompanying, follows from

ragah—attraction, attachment, passion

II, 8

duhkha anusayi dvesah

duhkha—pain, unhappiness, suffering

anusayi—dwells upon, accompanying, follows from

dvesah—(*dva* = divide + *sha* = life; to divide life) aversion, dislike, hatred

II, 9

svarasavahi vidusah api tatha rudhah abhinivesah

svarasavahi—sustained by an intrinsic force

vidusah—a wise, learned person

api—even

tatha—thus, also, in the same way

rudhah—dominating, rooted

abhinivesah—(*abhi* = moving toward + *ni* = liking + *esha* = life; the movement toward liking life) clinging to life, fear of death

II, 10

te prati-prasava heyah suksmah

te—they, these

prati-prasava—*practi* = against, reverse + *prasava* = procreation, generation = process of re-absorption, involution

heyah—reduced, destroyed, overcome

suksmah—subtle, potential

81

II, 11

dhyana heyas tad vrttayah

dhyana—meditation

heyas—reduced, destroyed, overcome

tad—those, their

vrttayah—(plural of *vrtti*) vacillation, variation, turning, twisting
   (*vrt* = to whirl)

II, 12

klesa mulah karma asayah drsta adrsta janma vedaniyah

klesa—primal causes of suffering, obstacles, afflictions

mulah—root, source

karma—action

asayah—reservoir of subliminal intentions, abode

drsta—seen, present, visible

adrsta—unseen, invisible, imperceptible, future

janma—births, lives

vedaniyah—to be experienced, known

II, 13

sati mule tad-vipako jaty-ayur bhogah

sati—existing, real

mule—root

tad—of it, that

vipako—mature, ripening, fruition

jaty—status in life, class

ayur—span of life, lifetime

bhogah—enjoyment, experiences

II, 14

te hlada paritapa phalah punya apunya hetutvat

te—these, they

hlada—joyful, delight

paritapa—sorrowful, distress, anguish

phalah—results, having fruits

punya—merit, virtuous

apunya—demerit, sin, vice

hetutvat—depending upon, on account of, being caused by

II, 15

parinama tapa samskara duhkaih guna vrtti virdohat ca duhkham eva sarvam vivekinah

parinama—consequence, result

tapa—torment, anxiety, anguish

samskara—subliminal impressions

duhkaih—pains, sorrow

guna—primal forces of desire

vrtti—vacillation, turning, twist (*vrt* = to whirl)

virdohat—due to opposition, contradictions, or conflict

ca—and

duhkham—misery, painful

eva—only, indeed

sarvam—all, whole

vivekinah—to the discriminating, enlightened

II, 16

heyam duhkham anagatam

heyam—avoidable, overcome, to be ended

duhkham—misery, pain

anagatam—future, not yet come

II, 17

drastri drishyayoh sanyogah heyah-hetuh

drastri—Seer

drishyayoh—the seen

sanyogah—close association, union, conjunction

heyah—to be ended, avoided

hetuh—cause, reason, purpose

II, 18

prakasa kriya sthiti silam bhuta indriya atmakam bhoga apavarga artham drsyam

prakasa—luminosity, intelligence, cognition

kriya—purification, means for attaining higher concentration

sthiti—steadiness, stability

silam—characteristics, qualities

bhuta—elements

indriya—sense organs

atmakam—embodied by, having the nature of

bhoga—enjoyment, pleasure

apavarga—liberation

artham—purpose, for the sake of

drsyam—the seen

II, 19

visesa avisesa lingamatra alingani guna-parvani

visesa—particular, specific, and visible

avisesa—non-specific and invisible

lingamatra—with form, marked

alingani—unformed, unmarked, without differentiating
      characteristics, unmanifest

guna-parvani—phases, stages of the primal forces of desire

II, 20

drasta drsi-matrah suddhah api pratyaya anupasyah

drasta—the Seer

drsi-matrah—seeing alone, consciousness only

suddhah—pure

api—even, though

pratyaya—thoughts directed toward an object, concept

anupasyah—witnessing, appears to see

II, 21

tadarthah eva drsyasya atma

tadarthah—for the purpose of, for the sake of that

eva—alone, solely

drsyasya—of the seen, of the knowable

atma—Self

II, 22

krtartham prati nastam api anastam tat anya sadharanatvat

krtartham—one whose purpose has been fulfilled, accomplished

prati—toward, for

nastam—ceased, non-existent, destroyed

api—although

anastam—not destroyed, existent

tat—of that, it

anya—other, to others

sadharanatvat—being normal, average, common

II, 23

sva svami saktyoh svarupa upalabdhi hetuh samyogah

sva—one's possessions

svami—owner, master

saktyoh—of the two powers

svarupa—own form, essential nature

upalabdhi—to obtain, outcome

hetuh—cause, reason, purpose

samyogah—association, coming together

II, 24

tasya hetuh avidya

tasya—its union

hetuh—cause

avidya—ignorance, lack of awareness of the True Self

II, 25

tad-abhavat samyoga-abhavah hanam tad-drseh kaivalyam

tad-abhavat—by the elimination of that (*avidya*)

samyoga—association, union, conjunction

abhavah—absence, disappearance

hanam—avoidance, remedy, end

tad-drseh—that of the Seer

kaivalyam—spiritual integration, absolute freedom, liberation

II, 26

viveka-khyatir aviplava hanopayah

viveka-khyatir—discriminative awareness

aviplava—unceasing, unbroken

hanopayah—means for remedy, avoidance, removal

II, 27

tasya saptadha pranta-bhumih prajna

tasya—its, of that

saptadha—sevenfold, seven phases

pranta—extremity, extends, boundary, final

bhumih—realm, ground, province

prajna—wisdom, insight

II, 28

yoganga anusthanat asuddhi ksaye jnana diptih avivekaka-khyateh

yoganga—component parts of yoga, limbs of yoga

anusthanat—sustained, devoted practice

asuddhi—impurity

ksaye—destruction, diminish, dwindle away

jnana—wisdom, spiritual knowledge

diptih—radiant light, shining forth

avivekaka—discriminative knowledge, distinction between Seer and seen

khyateh—identification

II, 29

yama niyama asana pranayama pratyahara dharana dhyana samadhayo astavangani

yama—self-control, self-restraint, moral principles

niyama—precepts, observances, fixed rules

asana—yoga pose

pranayama—regulation of prana, lengthening of the prana

pratyahara—withdrawal of the senses from their objects

dharana—contemplation, concentration

dhyana—meditation

samadhayo—absorption into Spirit

astavangani—eight component parts, limbs

II, 30

ahimsa satya asteya brahmacarya aprigrahah yamah

ahimsa—nonviolence, non-injury, harmlessness

satya—truthfulness, sincerity

asteya—freedom from stealing, misappropriating

brahmacarya—(*brahma* = Supreme Being + *carya* = living; living in the
    Supreme Being) search for, respect for the Divine, continence

aprigrahah—freedom from ownership, greed, non-acquisitiveness

yamah—self-control

II, 31

jati desa kala samaya anavacchinnah sarva-bhaumah maha-vratam

jati—status, class of birth, state of life

desa—place, country

kala—time

samaya—circumstance, condition

anavacchinnah—unlimited, unconditioned

sarva-bhaumah—universal

maha-vratam—great vow

II, 32

sauca santosa tapah svadhyaya Isvara-pranidhanani niyamah

sauca—purity, cleanliness

santosa—contentment

tapah—(*tap* = to heat intensively) self-discipline and purification, austerity

svadhyaya—(*sva* = Self, *adhyaya* = to go near; literally, to go near to yourself) self-study, observation aided through reflection on the scriptures

Isvara-pranidhanani—(*pra* = fullness, *ni* = under, *dhana* = placement; literally, placed under the fullness of the Lord) devotion or surrender to the Lord

niyamah—precepts, observances, fixed rules

II, 33

vitarka badhane pratipaksa bhavanam

vitarka—negative thoughts or emotions, unwholesome deliberations

badhane—on being disturbed, troubled by

pratipaksa—the opposite, contrary

bhavanam—cultivation, constant pondering, habitual thoughts

II, 34

vitarkah himsayah krta karita anumoditah lobha kordha moha
purvakah mrdu madhya adhimatrah duhkha ajnana ananta
phalah iti prtipaksa bhavanam

vitarkah—negative, unwholesome thoughts and emotions

himsayah—violent

krta—done by oneself

karita—done by others

anumoditah—permitted to be done

lobha—greed

kordha—anger

moha—delusion, confusion

purvakah—arising from, preceded by, caused by

mrdu—mild, slight

madhya—moderate

adhimatrah—excessive

duhkha—pain, sorrow, misery

ajnana—ignorance

ananta—infinite, endless

phalah—results, fruit

iti—thus, therefore

pratipaksa—opposites, contrary

bhavanam—cultivation, constant pondering, habitual thoughts

II, 35

ahimsa pratisthayam tat-sannidhau vaira tyagah

ahimsa—nonviolence

pratisthayam—on being firmly established, confirmed, abiding

tat-sannidhau—in its presence, vicinity

vaira—hostility, animosity

tyagah—ceases, abandonment

II, 36

satya pratisthayam kriya phalah asrayatvam

satya—truthfulness, sincerity

pratisthayam—on being firmly grounded, confirmed, abiding

kriya—actions to purify, means to a higher awareness

phalah—result, fruit

asrayatvam—become subservient, dependence upon

II, 37

asteya pratisthayam sarva ratna upasthanam

asteya—freedom from stealing, misappropriating, hoarding

pratisthayam—on being firmly grounded, confirmed, abiding

sarva—all

ratna—precious gems, prosperity, precious things

upasthanam—reveal, approach, acquire, gain

II, 38

brahma-carya pratisthayam virya labhah

brahma-carya—(*brahma* = Supreme Being + *carya* = living; living in the Supreme Being) search for, respect for the Divine, continence

pratisthayam—on being firmly grounded, abiding, confirmed

virya—inspired passion for life, vitality, vigor

labhah—acquire, gain

II, 39

aparigraha sthairye janma kathanta sambodhah

aparigraha—freedom from ownership, greed, possessiveness

sthairye—upon the foundation, on becoming steady

janma—birth

kathanta—the how, why, and wherefore, reasons

sambodhah—insight, understanding, knowledge

II, 40

saucat svanga jugupsa paraih asamsargah

saucat—from purity, owing to cleanliness

svanga—one's body, one's limbs

jugupsa—desire to protect, disinclination, indifference

paraih—with others

asamsargah—cessation, non-contamination, detachment

II, 41

sattva-suddhi saumanasya aikagrya indriya jaya atma-darsana
yogyatvani ca

sattva-suddhi—the purification of one's essence

saumanasya—cheerfulness, happiness of mind

aikagrya—one-pointedness

indriya—sense organs

jaya—mastery, control

atma-darsana—vision of the Self
yogyatvani—capability, fitness for
ca—and

II, 42

santosat anuttamah sukha labhah

santosat—from contentment
anuttamah—supreme, unexcelled
sukha—happiness
labhah—gain

II, 43

kaya indriya siddhih asuddhi ksayat tapasah

kaya—of the body
indriya—sense organs, senses
siddhih—attainment, powers of perfection
asuddhi—impurity
ksayat—dwindling, destruction, removal
tapasah—through self-discipline and purification, austerity,
    intensity of spiritual practice

II, 44

svadhyayat ista-devata samprayogah

svadhyayat—by self-study leading to self-knowledge, self-awareness
ista—beloved, personal, desired, choice
devata—shining one, deity
samprayogah—communion

II, 45

samadhi siddhih Isvara-pranidhanat

samadhi—absorption in Spirit
siddhih—supernatural powers, success
Isvara-pranidhanat—(*pra* = fullness, *ni* = under, *dhana* = placement;

91

placed under the fullness of the Lord) devotion or surrender
to the Lord

II, 46

sthira sukham asanam

sthira—stable, steady, steadfast

sukham—comfortable, easy, pleasant

asanam—(*as* = to be, to breathe + *san* = to put together with + *na*
= eternal cosmic vibration, happiness; to be put together
with the eternal cosmic vibration) yoga pose

II, 47

prayatna saithilya ananta samapattibhyam

prayatna—effort to overcome natural tendency for restlessness

saithilya—relaxation, lessening

ananta—(*ana* = breath) endless, infinite

samapattibhyam—merging with, identification with, assuming its
original form, conclusion

II, 48

tatah dvandva anabhighatah

tatah—from that

dvandva—pairs of opposites, duality

anabhighatah—ceases to be a disturbance, no impact, unconstrained

II, 49

tasmin sati svasa prasvasayoh gati vicchedah pranayamah

tasmin—upon this, on that

sati—having been accomplished, being acquired

svasa—inhalation

prasvasayoh—exhalation

gati—movement, flow

vicchedah—interruption, cessation, break

pranayamah—(*pra* = bring forth, *na* = eternal cosmic vibration, *ya* = really, yeah, *ma* = measure; to really bring forth a measure of the eternal cosmic vibration) regulation of prana, lengthening of the breath

II, 50

**bahya abhyantara stambha vrtteh desa kala samkhyabhih
paridrstah dirgha suksmah**

bahya—external, exhalation, emptying

abhyantara—internal, inhalation, filling

stambha—stationary, suppressed, restraint, retention

vrtteh—(*vrt* = to whirl) vacillation, turning, twist

desa—location, place

kala—time

samkhyabhih—and number

paridrstah—regulated, measured

dirgha—prolonged, long

suksmah—subtle, minute

II, 51

bahya abhyantara visaya aksepi caturthah

bahya—external, exhalation, emptying

abhyantara—internal, inhalation, filling

visaya—object, range, sphere

aksepi—transcends, passes over

caturthah—the fourth

II, 52

tatah ksiyate prakasa avaranam

tatah—as a result, then

ksiyate—dissolves, dispersed, disappears, destroyed

prakasa—supreme light, luminosity, radiance, light of the Self

avaranam—veil, covering

II, 53

dharanasu ca yogyata manasah

dharanasu—for contemplation, concentration

ca—and

yogyata—fitness, readiness

manasah—of the mind

II, 54

sva visaya asamprayoge cittasya svarupa anukarah
iva indriyanam pratyaharah

sva—one's own, their own

visaya—object

asamprayoge—not coming into contact, is displaced from

cittasya—the field of consciousness, the mind

svarupa—essential nature, own form

anukarah—imitation, follow

iva—as if, like

indriyanam—of the senses

pratyaharah—withdrawal

II, 55

tatah parama vashyata indriyanam

tatah—from that

parama—perfect, highest

vashyata—mastery, control

indriyanam—of the senses

CHAPTER III

VIBHUTI PADA

On Supernatural Abilities and Gifts

III, I

desa bandhah cittasya dharana

desa—place, point

bandhah—confining, fixation, binding

cittasya—of the mind, thought

dharana—contemplation, concentration

III, 2

tatra pratyaya ekatanata dhyanam

tatra—there, upon that, in that

pratyaya—foundation for directing thought to an object

ekatanata—continuity, single direction, uninterrupted flow

dhyanam—meditation

III, 3

tadeva artha matra nirbhasam svarupa sunyam iva samadhih

tadeva—(*tad* from the root *tat*, meaning that) the same, that
  specifically

artha—purpose, significance, wealth

matra—alone, only

nirbhasam—shining forth, reflecting, appearing

svarupa—own form, essence

sunyam—empty, void

iva—as if, as it were

samadhih—absorption in Spirit, communion with the essence
  of an object

95

III, 4

trayam ekatra samyamah

trayam—these three

ekatra—simultaneously, jointly, working together

samyamah—integrated, regulated consciousness

III, 5

tat-jayat prajna-alokah

tat—from that

jayat—by mastery

prajna—transcendental insight, intuitive knowledge, wisdom

alokah—light, brilliance, illumination

III, 6

tasya bhumisu viniyogah

tasya—its

bhumisu—gradual, in stages, in subtle states

viniyogah—progression, application

III, 7

trayam antarangam purvebhyah

trayam—these three

antarangam—inner limbs, internal parts

purvebhyah—in contrast to the earlier ones, distinct from those
previous

III, 8

tadapi bahirangam nirbijasya

tadapi—even that, they also

bahirangam—external limbs, outer parts

nirbijasya—of the seedless (*nirbija*) samadhi

III, 9

**vyutthana nirodha samskaryah abhibhava pradurbhavau
nirodha-ksana citta-anvayah nirodha-parinamah**

vyutthana—emergence of thoughts, outgoing thought

nirodha—cease, restraint

samskaryah—subliminal impressions

abhibhava—disappearance, submergence, suppression

pradurbhavau—appearance, emergence

nirodha—cease, restraint

ksana—moment

citta—consciousness, mind, thought

anvayah—association, connection

nirodha—cease, restraint

parinamah—transformation

III, 10

tasya prasanta vahina samskarat

tasya—of that, its

prasanta—peaceful, tranquil

vahina—flow

samskarat—by repeated habit, frequent repetition

III, 11

**sarvarthata ekagratayah ksaya udayau cittasya
samadhi-parinamah**

sarvarthata—many-pointedness, distracted mind

ekagratayah—one-pointedness

ksaya—decay, disappearance

udayau—arising, appearance

cittasya—of the mind

samadhi—absorption into Spirit

parinamah—transformation

III, 12

tatah punah santa uditau tulya pratyayau cittasya
ekagrata-parinamah

tatah—then, from that

punah—again

santa—subsided, quieted

uditau—manifest, arisen

tulya—equal

pratyayau—thoughts that direct awareness, content of the mind

cittasya—of the mind, thought

ekagrata—one-pointedness

parinamah—transformation

III, 13

etena bhutendriyesu dharma laksana avastha
parinamah vyakhayatah

etena—by this

bhuta—elements

indriyesu—in regard to the senses

dharma—quality, property

laksana—character

avastha—condition

parinamah—transformation

vyakhayatah—explained

III, 14

santa udita avyapadesya dharma anupati dharmi

santa—latent, subsided

udita—manifest, arisen

avyapadesya—unmanifested, indistinguishable

dharma—quality, property

anupati—correlated to, common to

dharmi—substratum of qualities

III, 15

krama anyatvam parinama anyatve hetuh

krama—order, sequential progression, natural law

anyatvam—variation, difference, separateness

parinama—transformation

anyatve—in variation, for separateness

hetuh—reason, cause

III, 16

parinama traya samyamat atita anagata-jnanam

parinama—transformations

traya—the three

samyamat—by practicing, performing samyama

atita—past

anagata—future

jnanam—knowledge

III, 17

sabda artha pratyayanam itare-taradhyasat sankarahtat-
pravibhaga samyamat sarva bhuta ruta-jnanam

sabda—-word, sound, nature

artha—meaning, object, wealth

pratyayanam—ideas, thoughts that direct awareness, mind's content

itare-taradhyasat—due to mental superimposition

sankarah—confusion, mixed together

tat-pravibhaga—their distinction, separation

samyamat—by practicing, performing samyama

sarva—all

bhuta—living beings

ruta—speech, sounds

jnanam—knowledge

III, 18

samskara saksat-karanat purva-jati jnanam

samskara—subliminal impressions

saksat—direct

karanat—perception

purva—previous

jati—births

jnanam—knowledge

III, 19

pratyayasya para-citta-jnanam

pratyayasya—on the content of the mind, perception

para—another

citta—mind, point of view, thought

jnanam—knowledge, wisdom

III, 20

na ca tat salambanam tasya avisayi bhutatvat

na—not

ca—and

tat—that, its

salambanam—with support

tasya—of that, its

avisayi—unperceived, not the object of thought

bhutatvat—due to its nature of being

III, 21

kaya rupa samyamat tad-grahya-sakti stambhe caksuh prakasa
asamprayoge antardhanam

kaya—body

rupa—form

samyamat—by doing, practicing samyama

tad—its, that

grahya—receptive

sakti—power, capacity

stambhe—suspension

caksuh—eye

prakasa—illumination, light, luminous

asamprayoge—absence of contact

antardhanam—invisibility, disappearance

III, 22

etena sabda-adi antardhanam uktam

etena—by this

sabda—sound, name, word

adi—and others

antardhanam—disappearance

uktam—has been described, said

III, 23

sopakramam nirupakramam ca karma tatsamyamat
aparanta-jnanam artisebhyah va

sopakramam—has an immediate effect, result, maturing in a short
time

nirupakramam—results after a long time, dormant karma

ca—and

karma—action

tatsamyamat—practicing samyama on them

aparanta—death

jnanam—knowledge

artisebhyah—by omens, signs

va—or

III, 24

maitry-adisu balani

maitry—(by *samyama*) on friendliness

adisu—and other (virtues)

balani—strengths, powers

III, 25

balesu hasti baladini

balesu—(by *samyama*) on the strength, powers

hasti—elephant

baladini—strength and other qualities

III, 26

pravrtti aloka nyasat suksma vyavahita viprakrsta-jananam

pravrtti—higher sensory knowledge, supersensory perception

aloka—light, brilliance

nyasat—by projecting, directing

suksma—subtle, fine

vyavahita—hidden, concealed, obscure

viprakrsta—distant, remote

jananam—knowledge

III, 27

bhuvana-jnanam surve samyamat

bhuvana—solar system, worlds, regions of existence

jnanam—knowledge

surve—on the Sun

samyamat—by performing *samyama*

III, 28

candre tara-vyuha-jnanam

candre—(by doing *samyama*) on the Moon

tara—of the stars, stellar

vyuha—organization, arrangement

jnanam—knowledge

III, 29

dhruve tad-gati-jnanam

dhruve—(by doing *samyama*) on the Pole Star
tad—from that
gati—movement, motion
jnanam—knowledge

III, 30

nabhi-cakre kaya-vyuha-jnanam

nabhi—(by practicing *samyama*) on the navel
cakre—*chakra*, energy or psychic center
kaya—the body
vyuha—organization, arrangement, constitution
jnanam—knowledge

III, 31

kantha-kupe ksut-pipasa nivrttih

kantha—(by practicing *samyama*) on the throat
kupe—well, pit, cavity
ksut—hunger
pipasa—thirst
nivrttih—ceases, disappears, subdued

III, 32

kurma-nadyam sthairyam

kurma—(by practicing *samyama*) on the tortoise-shaped
nadyam—tube, subtle channel (in the neck region)
sthairyam—motionlessness

III, 33

murdha-jyotisi siddha-darsanam

murdha—(by practicing *samyama*) on the crown of the head

jyotisi—on the light

siddha—perfected masters, adepts

darsanam—vision of, spiritual vision

III, 34

pratibhat va sarvam

pratibhat—(by practicing *samyama*) on intuition, from a flash of illumination, intuitive perception

va—or

sarvam—everything, all knowledge

III, 35

hrdaye citta-samvit

hrdaye—(by practicing *samyama*) on the heart

citta—thought, mind

samvit—full knowledge

III, 36

sattva purusayoh atyanta-samkirnayoh pratyaya avisesah bhogah pararthatvat svartha-samyamat purusa-jnanam

sattva—pure being, clarity of mind, lucidity

purusayoh—of the transcendental Self

atyanta—extremely, absolutely

samkirnayoh—distinct

pratyaya—awareness, thought that directs awareness

avisesah—nondistinct, doesn't distinguish

bhogah—experience, sensual enjoyment

pararthatvat—separate, apart, distinct from another

svartha—self-interest, its own sake

samyamat—by practicing samyama on

purusa—the Self

jnanam—knowledge

III, 37

tatah pratibha sravana vedana adarsa asvada vartah jayante

tatah—these, from it

pratibha—spiritual perceptions, flash of illumination, intuitive insight

sravana—Divine, supersensory, transcendental hearing

vedana—Divine, supersensory, transcendental touch

adarsa—Divine, supersensory, transcendental vision, sight

asvada—Divine, supersensory, transcendental taste

vartah—Divine, supersensory, transcendental aroma

jayante—occurs, produced, are born

III, 38

te samadhau upasargah vyutthane siddhayah

te—these, they

samadhau—in samadhi, spiritual absorption

upasargah—obstacles, impediments

vyutthane—to worldly pursuits, to an outgoing mind, worldly minded

siddhayah—attainments, perfections, powers

III, 39

bahdha-karana saithilyat pracara samvedanat
ca cittasya para-sarira-avesah

bahdha—bondage

karana—cause

saithilyat—relaxation, loosening

pracara—pathways, movements, passage

samvedanat—from sensitivity, knowing

ca—and

cittasya—of the mind, thought, perception

para—another

sarira—into the body

avesah—entry

III, 40

udanajayat jala panka kanta-kadisu asangah utkrantih ca

udana—(*ud* = upward), a form of *prana* centered in the throat that
  moves upward to the head and beyond

jayat—by mastery

jala—water

panka—mud, mire

kanta—thorns

kadisu—and so on, etc.

asangah—no contact

utkrantih—levitation, ascension, rising up

ca—and

III, 41

samana-jayat jvalanam

samana—(*sama* = equal, same) equalizing air, a form of *prana*
  centered in the small intestine that promotes digestion by its
  centrifugal force

jayat—by mastery

jvalanam—radiance, blazing, shine

III, 42

srotra akasayoh samdandha samyamat divyam srotram

srotra—of hearing, of the ear

akasayoh—space/ether

samdandha—inter-relationship

samyamat—by practicing *samyama*

divyam—divine

srotram—organ of hearing, power of hearing

III, 43

kaya akasayoh sambandha samyamat laghu-tula-samapatteh
ca akasa-gamanam

kaya—body

akasayoh—of space/ether
sambandha—relation
samyamat—by practicing *samyama*
laghu—light
tula—cotton
samapatteh—by creating a rapport, fusion, becoming one with
ca—and
akasa—space, ether, sky
gamanam—going through, movement

III, 44

bahih akalpita vrttih maha-videha tatah prakasa avarana-ksayah

bahih—external, outside
akalpita—unimaginable, inconceivable
vrttih—vacillation, turning, twist (*vrt* = to whirl)
maha—great
videha—out-of-body, disembodied
tatah—from that
prakasa—light, illumination
avarana—covering
ksayah—disperse, disappearance, wasting away

III, 45

**sthula svarupa suksma anvaya artha-vatva
samyamat bhutajayah**

sthula—gross state
svarupa—fundamental, essential nature, intrinsic
suksma—subtle state
anvaya—interpenetrating, all-pervasive
artha—wealth, abundance
vatva—function, serving the purpose
samyamat—by practicing *samyama*
bhutajayah—mastery of the elements

III, 46

tatah animadi pradurbhavah kayasampat
taddharma anabhighatah ca

tatah—from this

animadi—to become small, minute, and other attainments

pradurbhavah—appearance

kayasampat—*kaya* = body; *sampat* = wealth, perfection

taddharma—of its functions, attributes

anabhighatah—non-obstruction, not being overcome, immune

ca—and

III, 47

rupa lavanya bala vajra samhanavatvani kayasampat

rupa—beauty, graceful form, form

lavanya—gracefulness, fine complexion

bala—strength

vajra—qualities of a diamond; hardness, robustness

samhanavatvani—firmness, extraordinary endurability

kayasampat—*kaya* = body; *sampat* = wealth, perfection

III, 48

grahana svarupa asmita anvaya arthavattva
samyamat indriya-jayah

grahana—directing perception, act of perceiving

svarupa—essential nature

asmita—egoism, sense of "I am"

anvaya—conjunction, all-pervasiveness

arthavattva—reason for being, purpose

samyamat—by practicing *samyama*

indriya—senses, sense organs

jayah—mastery

III, 49

tatah manojavitvam vikarana bhavah pradhana-jayah ca

tatah—from it, this, therefrom

manojavitvam—swiftness, speed like that of thought

vikarana—freedom from the senses, independent of sense organs

bhavah—feeling, state, attitude

pradhana—primary cause, original matter

jayah—mastery

ca—and

III, 50

sattva purusa anyata khyati-matrasya sarva-bhava
adhisthatrtvam sarvajnatrtvam ca

sattva—purity of mind, brilliance, pure beingness

purusa—True Self

anyata—difference, distinction, separateness

khyati—identification, awareness

matrasya—only, for only, of that

sarva—all

bhava—states, manifestations

adhisthatrtvam—supremacy

sarvajnatrtvam—omniscience

ca—and

III, 51

tadvairagyat api dosa-bija-ksaye kaivalyam

tadvairagyat—from non-attachment to that, by renunciation

api—even, also

dosa—bondage, defects, imperfections

bija—seed

ksaye—upon the disappearance, dwindling

kaivalyam—spiritual integration, absolute freedom, liberation

III, 52

sthany-upanimantrane sanga-smaya-akaranam
punar-anista prasangat

sthany—high-placed, presiding celestial beings

upanimantrane—on being respectfully invited, admired, enticed

sanga—attachment, pleasure, contact

smaya—pride

akaranam—without cause, avoidance, not accepting

punar—again

anista—undesirable, unfavorable

prasangat—recurrence, revival, due to inclination

III, 53

ksana tat kramayoh samyamat vivekajam jnanam

ksana—moment, instant

tat—its

kramayoh—order of succession, sequence

samyamat—by practicing *samyama*

vivekajam—born of discrimination, realization, discernment

jnanam—knowledge

III, 54

jati laksana desaih anyata anavacchedat tulyayoh tatah
pratipattih

jati—birth, class, origin

laksana—distinctive characteristics

desaih—position, place

anyata—separateness, difference

anavacchedat—indistinguishable, not restricted, undefined

tulyayoh—of similars, two similar objects

tatah—from it, from this

pratipattih—understanding, ascertainment

III, 55

tarakam sarva-visayam sarvatha-visayam akramam ca iti
vivekajam jnanam

tarakam—that which helps one "cross over," transcendent, liberator

sarva—all

visayam—objects

sarvatha—all conditions, at all times

visayam—objects

akramam—without sequence or succession, orderless

ca—and

iti—that is all, thus, therefore

vivekajam—born of discrimination

jnanam—knowledge

III, 56

sattva purusayoh suddhi samye kaivlyam iti

sattva—purity of mind, pure beingness

purusayoh—of the transcendental Self

suddhi—purity, purification

samye—on becoming equal

kaivlyam—spiritual integration, freedom, liberation

iti—thus, therefore, that's all

CHAPTER IV

KAIVALYA PADA

On Absolute Freedom

IV, 1

janma ausadhi mantra tapah samadhijah siddhayah

janma—birth

ausadhi—magical herbs

mantra—mantra, revered words whose repetition produces specific results

tapah—(*tap* = to heat intensively) intense spiritual practice, austerity, heat

samadhijah– born of *samadhi*

siddhayah—supernatural abilities, attainments, powers

IV, 2

jatyantara parinamah prakrty-apurat

jatyantara—into another birth, class

parinamah—transformation

prakrty—primal nature

apurat—by overflowing, abundant flow

IV, 3

**nimittam aprayojakam prakrtinam varana-bhedah
tu tatah ksetrikavat**

nimittam—incidental cause, instrumental, tool

aprayojakam—indirectly causing

prakrtinam—of natural tendencies

varana—obstacle, barrier, cover

bhedah—removal, separating

tu—but, on the other hand

tatah—from that
ksetrikavat—like a farmer

IV, 4

nirmana-cittani asmit-amatrat

nirmana—fabricated, created, can be produced
cittani—minds, thoughts
asmit—sense of individuality, ego
amatrat—from that alone, primary, solely

IV, 5

pravrtti bhede prayojakam cittam ekam anekesam

pravrtti—activity, functions
bhede—multiplicity, difference, diversity
prayojakam—motivator, directing, originator
cittam—mind, thought
ekam—one
anekesam—diversity, numerous, innumerable

IV, 6

tatra dhyanajam anasayam

tatra—of them, these
dhyanajam—born of meditation
anasayam—free from accumulation of impressions, free of residue

IV, 7

karma asukla akrsnam yoginah trividham itaresam

karma—action
asukla—not white
akrsnam—not black
yoginah—of a yogi
trividham—threefold
itaresam—for others, in the case of others

IV, 8

tatah tad-vipaka anugunanam eva abhivyaktih vasananam

tatah—from that, of these

tad—that, it

vipaka—ripening, maturation

anugunanam—accordingly, correspondingly

eva—only, alone

abhivyaktih—proceeding, manifestation

vasananam—(*vi* = not being steady, perfume) subliminal desires, residual impressions, tendencies

IV, 9

jati desa kala vyavahitanam api anantaryam smrti samskarayoh ekarupatvat

jati—birth, class, station of life

desa—place

kala—time

vyavahitanam—separated, divided

api—although, even

anantaryam—continuity, immediate succession, sequence

smrti—memory

samskarayoh—subliminal impressions

ekarupatvat—identity, uniformity, same appearance

IV, 10

tasam anaditvam ca asisah nityatvat

tasam—of these, there is

anaditvam—without beginning

ca—and

asisah—primordial will, the will to live

nityatvat—due to an eternal nature, by permanence

IV, 11

hetu phala asraya alambanaih sangrhitatvat esam
abhave tad abhavah

hetu—cause, motive

phala—effect, result

asraya—support, basis, substratum

alambanaih—supported object, depending upon

sangrhitatvat—inseparable, held together, being bound together

esam—of these

abhave—in absence, upon the disappearance

tad—them

abhavah—vanish, their disappearance

IV, 12

atita anagatam svarupatah asti adhvabhedat dharmanam

atita—past

anagatam—future

svarupatah—in its essential form, true form

asti—exists

adhvabhedat—owing to differences

dharmanam—characteristics, properties

IV, 13

te vyakta suksmah gunatmanah

te—they, these

vyakta—manifest

suksmah—subtle and unmanifested

gunatmanah—having the quality of nature's primal forces

IV, 14

parinama ekatvat vastu-tattvam

parinama—transformation, change, modification

ekatvat—due to oneness, unity

115

vastu—object
tattvam—essence, reality

IV, 15

vastu-samye citta-bhedat tayoh vibhaktah panthah

vastu—in the case of the external object
samye—being the same
citta—mind, thought
bhedat—owing to differences
tayoh—of these two, of both, their
vibhaktah—separate, distinct, different
panthah—paths, ways of being

IV, 16

na ca ekacitta tantram vastu tat apramanakam tada kim syat

na—not
ca—and
ekacitta—one mind, thought
tantram—dependent
vastu—object
tat—that
apramanakam—unrecognized
tada—then
kim—what
syat—could be, would happen, would exist

IV, 17

tad-uparaga apeksitvat cittasya vastu jnata ajnatam

tad—by that
uparaga—coloring, conditioning, contact, reflection
apeksitvat—due to the dependency
cittasya—of thought, mind
vastu—object

jnata—known

ajnatam—unknown

IV, 18

sada jnatah citta-vrttayah tatprabhoh purusasya aparinamitvat

sada—always

jnatah—known

citta—thought, mind, perception (*cit* = to perceive, be bright)

vrttayah—vacillation, turning, twist (*vrt* = to whirl)

tatprabhoh—its lord, master

purusasya—of the transcendental Self

aparinamitvat—due to the changelessness, constancy

IV, 19

na tat svabhasam drsyatvat

na—not

tat—that, it

svabhasam—self-illumination

drsyatvat—because it is knowable, being an object

IV, 20

ekasamaye ca ubhaya anavadharanam

ekasamaye—simultaneously

ca—and

ubhaya—both

anavadharanam—cannot perceive, incomprehensible

IV, 21

cittantaradrsye buddhibuddheh atiprasangah smrtisankarah ca

cittantaradrsye—one mind being known by another

buddhibuddheh—cognition of cognitions

atiprasangah—absurdity

smrtisankarah—confusion of impressions

ca—and

IV, 22

citeh apratisamkramayah tad-akara-pattau sva-buddhi-samvedanam

citeh—the Self, awareness of Self

apratisamkramayah—not passing from one to another, changeless

tad—its, in that

akara—form

pattau—by getting the reflection of the Self, having the appearance

sva—one's own, its own

buddhi—evolved consciousness, higher intelligence,
      wisdom principle

samvedanam—knowing, experience, identifies with, assumes

IV, 23

drastr drsya uparaktam cittam sarvartham

drastr—the Seer, knower

drsya—the known, seen

uparaktam—colored

cittam—awareness, thought, perception

sarvartham—all inclusive, understands all, all objects

IV, 24

**tat asankhyeya vasanabhih citram api parartham
samhatya-karitvat**

tat—that

asankhyeya—innumerable, countless

vasanabhih—through subtle desires, impressions

citram—variegated

api—although

parartham—for the sake of the Self

samhatya—collaboration, closely allied

karitvat—because of, on account of

IV, 25

vesesa-darsinah atmabhava bhavana-nivrttih

vesesa—distinction

darsinah—of one who sees, the Seer

atmabhava—self-consciousness, self-centeredness

bhavana—reflection, feeling, dwelling upon in the mind

nivrttih—complete cessation, discontinuation, inactivity

IV, 26

tada vivekanimnam kaivalya prag-bharam cittam

tada—then

vivekanimnam—inclination toward discrimination

kaivalya—absolute freedom, liberation

prag—toward

bharam—gravitates, pulls irresistibly

cittam—awareness, thought, perception

IV, 27

tat cchidresu pratyaya-antarani samskarebhyah

tat—these, that

cchidresu—in the intervals, in the breaks in between

pratyaya—distracting thoughts, thoughts directed to objects

antarani—other

samskarebhyah—from impressions, from habituation

IV, 28

hanam esam klesavat uktam

hanam—destruction, removal, cessation

esam—of these, their

klesavat—like the obstructions, obstacles (*kleshas*)

uktam—described, is said

IV, 29

prasamkhyane api akusidasya sarvatha vivekahyateh
dharmameghah samadhih

prasamkhyane—in the highest meditation, realization, discrimination
api—even
akusidasya—one who has no interest left, totally disinterested in selfish motives
sarvatha—constant, in every way
vivekahyateh—discriminative discernment, discrimination
dharmameghah—(*mih* = to make water) cloud of virtue, showering of righteousness (*dharma*)
samadhih—absorbed in Spirit, communion

IV, 30

tatah klesa karma nivrttih

tatah—from that
klesa—obstacles, afflictions
karma—law of karma, action
nivrttih—cessation, discontinuation, inactivity

IV, 31

tada sarva avarana mala-petasya jnanasya anantyat
jneyam alpam

tada—then
sarva—all
avarana—covering, that which obscures, veils
mala—impurities, imperfections
petasya—removed, freed of
jnanasya—of knowledge
anantyat—due to the endless, infinity
jneyam—the known, knowable, objective universe
alpam—but little, nothing, trivial

Mukunda Stiles

IV, 32

tatah krtarthanam parinama-krama samptih gunanam

tatah—thereafter, then

krtarthanam—having fulfilled their purpose

parinama—transformation, of the changes

krama—series, succession, sequence, process

samptih—conclusion, terminate

gunanam—primal natural forces, qualities (*gunas*)

IV, 33

ksana pratiyogi parinama aparanta nirgrahyah kramah

ksana—moment

pratiyogi—corresponding, uninterrupted sequence

parinama—transformation, evolutionary changes

aparanta—at the end, in the end

nirgrahyah—recognized as distinct, entirely grasped

kramah—series, sequence, succession

IV, 34

purusartha sunyanam gunanam pratiprasavah kaivalyam
svarupa-pratistha va citisaktih iti

purusartha—purpose of the True Self, wealth/aims of life

sunyanam—devoid of

gunanam—of the primal natural forces, qualities (*gunas*)

pratiprasavah—involution, re-absorption

kaivalyam—spiritual integration, absolute freedom, liberation

svarupa—real or essential nature

pratistha—establishment, abidance

va—or

citisaktih—the power of consciousness

iti—the end, finis

Sources

❦

Primary Sources for Sanskrit Translations

Baba Hari Dass. *Yoga Sutras of Patanjali: Chapter One—Samadhi Pada.* Santa Cruz, CA: Sri Rama Publishing, 2001.

Basu, Major B. D., ed. Rama Prasada, trans. *Patanjali's Yoga Sutras—Sacred Books of the Hindus.* vol. iv. Allahabad, India: Sudhindranath Vasu, 1924.

Bouanchaud, Bernard. *The Essence of Yoga.* Portland, OR: Rudra Press, 1997.

Shri Brahmananda Sarasvati (Rammurti Mishra). *The Textbook of Yoga Philosophy.* New York: Julian Press, 1987.

Feuerstein, Georg. *The Yoga Sutra of Patanjali.* Rochester, VT: Inner Traditions International, 1989.

Govindan, Marshall. *Kriya Yoga Sutras of Patanjali and the Siddhas.* Eastman, Quebec: Kriya Yoga Publications, 2000.

Houston, Vyaas. *The Yoga Sutra Workbook—The Certainty of Freedom.* Warwick, NY: American Sanskrit Institute, 1995.

Iyengar, B. K. S. *Light on the Yoga Sutras of Patanjali.* San Francisco: Aquarian/Thorsons, 1993.

Karambelkar, P. V. *Patanjali's Yoga Sutras.* Lonavla, India: Yoga Mimamsa Publications, 1978.

Swami Satchidananda. *Patanjali's Yoga Sutras.* Yogaville, VA: Integral Yoga Publications, 1991.

Swami Satyananda Saraswati. *Four Chapters on Freedom—Commentary on Yoga Sutras of Patanjali.* Munger, Bihar, India: Bihar School of Yoga, 1989.

Taimni, I. K. *The Science of Yoga.* Wheaton, IL: Theosophical Publishing House, 1967.

Secondary Sources *(without word-for-word translations)*

Bangali Baba. *The Yoga Sutra of Patanjali* with the commentary of Vyasa. Delhi: Motilal Banarsidass, 1979.

Coster, Geraldine. *Yoga and Western Psychology.* Delhi: Motilal Banarsidass, 1934, 1968.

122

Desikachar, T. K. V. *The Heart of Yoga*. Rochester, VT: Inner Traditions International, 1995.

Dvivedi, Manilal Nabhubhai. *The Yoga-Sutra of Patanjali*. Bombay: Rajaram Tukaram Pub. for the Bombay Theosophical Publication Fund, 1914.

Gherwal, Rishi Singh. *Patanjali's Raja Yoga*. Santa Barbara, CA: Rishi Singh Gherwal, 1935.

Ghosh, Shyam. *The Original Yoga as Expounded in Siva-Samhita, Gheranda-Samhita and Patanjala Yoga-sutra*. New Delhi: Munshiram Manoharlal Publishers Pvt. Ltd. , 1980.

Iyengar, B. K. S. *Yoga Sutra of Patanjali*. Poona, India: Ramamani Iyengar Memorial Yoga Institute, 1987.

Johnston, Charles. *The Yoga Sutras of Patanjali*. London: Watkins Publishing, 1912, 1975.

Miller, Barbara Stoler. *Yoga: Discipline of Freedom*. New York: Bantam Books, 1998.

Swami Hariharananda Aranya. *Yoga Philosophy of Patanjali*. Albany: SUNY Press, 1983.

Swami Prabhavananda and Christopher Isherwood. *How to Know God: The Yoga Aphorisms of Patanjali*. New York: Mentor Books, 1969.

Swami Shyam. *Patanjali Yog Darshan*. Montreal: Be All Publications, 1980.

Swami Venkatesananda. *Enlightened Living—A New Interpretative Translation of the Yoga Sutra of Maharshi Patanjali*. Delhi: Motilal Banarsidass, 1978.

Swami Vivekananda. *Raja Yoga or Conquering the Inner Nature*. London: Longmans, Green and Co. , 1912.

Tatya, Tookaram. *The Yoga Philosophy*. Bombay: Theosophical Society Publications, 1885.

Woods, James Haughton. *The Yoga-System of Patanjali*. Delhi: Motilal Banarsidass, 1977.

BOOKS ABOUT THE *YOGA SUTRAS* AND YOGA PHILOSOPHY

Anirvan. *Inner Yoga (Antaryoga)*. New Delhi: Voice of India, 1995.

Bernard, Theo. *Hindu Philosophy*. New York: Philosophical Library, 1947.

123

Besant, Annie. *An Introduction to Yoga.* Madras: Theosophical Publishing House, 1913.

Bragdon, Claude. *An Introduction to Yoga.* London: Kegan Paul, Trench, Trubner & Co., Ltd., 1933.

Crowley, Aleister. *Eight Lectures on Yoga.* Dallas, TX: Sangreal Foundation, 1972.

Dasgupta, Surendranath. *Yoga as Philosophy and Religion.* Delhi: Motilal Banarsidass, 1978.

————. *Yoga Philosophy In Relation to Other Systems of Indian Thought.* Delhi: Motilal Banarsidass, 1979.

Desikachar, T. K. V. with Cravens, R. H. *Health, Healing and Beyond. Yoga and the Living Tradition of Krishnamacharya.* New York: Aperture, 1998.

Eliade, Mircea. *Patanjali and Yoga.* New York: Schocken Books, 1975.

Feuerstein, Georg. *The Philosophy of Classical Yoga.* Rochester, VT: Inner Traditions International, 1996.

————. *The Shambhala Encyclopedia of Yoga.* Boston: Shambhala, 2000.

————. *The Yoga Tradition.* Prescott, AZ: Hohm Press, 1998.

Frawley, David. *Ayurveda and the Mind.* Twin Lakes, WI: Lotus Press, 1996.

————. *Yoga and Ayurveda.* Twin Lakes, WI: Lotus Press, 1999.

Puri, B. N. *India in the Time of Patanjali.* Bharatiya Vidya Bhavan, 1968.

Ramaswami, Srivatsa. *Yoga for the Three Stages of Life.* Rochester, VT: Inner Traditions International, 2000.

Slater, Wallace. *Raja Yoga: A Simplified and Practical Course.* Wheaton, IL: Quest Books, 1968.

Swami Chidananda. *Path to Blessedness—Quintessence of the Ashtanga Yoga of Sage Maharshi Patanjali.* Shivanandanagar: Divine Life Society Publication, 1991.

Swami Rama. *Lectures on Yoga.* Honesdale, PA. : Himalayan International Institute, 1979.

Swami Venkatesananda. *Lectures on Raja Yoga.* Capetown, South Africa: Chiltern Yoga Trust, 1972.

Tyberg, Judith M. *The Language of the Gods—Sanskrit Keys to India's Wisdom.* Los Angeles: East-West Cultural Center, 1970.